Praise for Preparing the Pastors We Need

"Amidst constant talk about changing church, George Mason brings us the rich wisdom of pastors and congregations called to prepare new ministers. This is a practical, sophisticated how-to book wrapped in a love letter. Mason's passion for ministry and his profound, tender respect for the congregation shine through."

Melissa Wiginton, Education Beyond the Walls at Austin Seminary

"If churches were like cars, they would have a built-in glove compartment. This book would go in it. George Mason has assembled a concise manual to help healthy congregations know how to shape a new generation of wise and gifted pastors. The model is superb. Mason's ideas are right on the money."

Peter W. Marty, pastor, St. Paul Lutheran Church, Davenport, Iowa

"There are plenty of books that tell us what we already know about doing and being church in the 21st century—churches are dying on the vine and in our communities. There is no more desperate time for quality and qualified pastors than right now. In *Preparing the Pastors We Need,* George Mason provides a refreshing and thoughtful approach and strategy to address the critical issues of leadership and its healthy generation for the future church."

Gary V. Simpson, senior pastor, Concord Baptist Church of Christ, Brooklyn, New York, and associate professor of homiletics, Drew Theological Seminary

"George Mason draws on his own experience, and the experience of others, to make a compelling case for the importance of pastoral residency programs. He also explains, in clear and helpful ways, how to establish and support such a ministry. But this book also is something more—an invaluable resource for anyone interested in helping new clergy make the transition from classroom to parish."

Martin B. Copenhaver, senior pastor of Wellesley Congregational Church (United Church of Christ) and co-author, with Lillian Daniel, of This Odd and Wondrous Calling.

"That seminary education is necessary but not sufficient preparation for pastoral ministry is now assumed. What remains to be worked out is how learning in and through the practice of ministry in the life of congregations happens. George Mason has lived the how and in *Preparing the Pastors We Need,* he gives us the practical wisdom we need to be pastors and congregations sufficient to the task of raising up a new generation of pastoral leaders."

David J. Wood, senior minister of Glencoe Union Church and former Coordinator of the Lilly Endowment–funded Transition into Ministry Program

Preparing the
Pastors We Need

Preparing the Pastors We Need

RECLAIMING THE CONGREGATION'S ROLE IN TRAINING CLERGY

George Mason

Foreword by Christopher Coble

Alban Institute
Herndon, Virginia

The Alban Institute
2121 Cooperative Way, Suite 100
Herndon, VA 20171

Unless otherwise noted, all Scripture quotations are from the New Revised Standard Version of the Bible, copyright © 1989, Division of Christian Education of the National Council of the Churches of Christ in the United States of America, and are used by permission.

Library of Congress Cataloging-in-Publication Data
Mason, George.
    Preparing the pastors we need : reclaiming the congregation's role in training clergy / George Mason.
        p. cm.
Includes bibliographical references (p. 165).
    ISBN 978-1-56699-427-9
    1. Clergy--Training of. 2. Christian leadership. 3. Church--Teaching office. I. Title.
    BV4020.M348 2012
    253.071'55--dc23
                                    2012023981

12   13   14   15   16   VG   5   4   3   2   1

In grateful memory of
C. Bruce McIver,
pastor, mentor, and friend

Contents

Foreword

Taking on the leadership of a congregation is daunting, and the new mantle of leadership can feel awkward on the shoulders of new pastors. Preaching weekly, leading worship services, teaching the faith to children and adults, comforting the sick and dying, guiding the work of committees, managing a congregation's business, supervising staff, motivating volunteers, representing the church at community events—the list of pastoral duties is long. When they put on their clerical robes for the first time and take charge of their first congregations, new pastors experience many disorienting moments as they learn to identify priorities and to juggle their multiple tasks and responsibilities.

Seasoned pastors, on the other hand, carry with them a sense of confidence and move seamlessly from task to task and from one ministry setting to the next. Leading a prayer service, working with a local contractor on a church building issue, studying for an upcoming sermon, sharing a comforting word at a hospital bed, teaching a confirmation class, mediating a disagreement between two church members, writing a meditation for a newsletter and attending a high school musical performance—they juggle all of these activities and more on a typical day.

Ask veteran pastors about their early years in ministry, however, and just about everyone will talk about the difficulty of their first years and the important lessons they learned in their first congregations. They will tell you stories about mistakes and missed opportunities and awkward moments when they did not know what to do next. But they will express gratitude for patient lay leaders and wise mentors who helped them discover their gifts as well as their limitations and showed them how to structure their time so they would not be so overwhelmed by the demands of the day. They will talk about moments in their crucial early years when they came to understand more deeply the character of pastoral work and to learn how to sort out and respond to the demands placed upon them. These experiences helped them develop an internal pastoral gyroscope that would shape their leadership practices and keep them centered within the whirlwind of congregational life day in and day out, year in and year out.

How does this happen? How do new pastors develop this capacity? What helps them make successful transitions from seminary classrooms to congregational pulpits? What does it look like when this transition goes well?

In 1999, Lilly Endowment launched its Transition into Ministry (TiM) initiative. With support from Endowment grants, 38 organizations have taken up these questions by designing and testing innovative leadership development programs for new pastors. These programs are a key element in the Endowment's overall effort to enhance the quality of pastoral leadership in Christian congregations and parishes.

Why concentrate on this transition? Before launching the TiM initiative, we spoke with scores of pastors about their ministries and what prepared them best to lead congregations. Veteran clergy, not surprisingly, talked about their early years of ministry and told us about mentors and pastoral peers who helped them work through transition issues and difficult congregational situations. These colleagues and partners in ministry played critical roles in teaching them the practices of pastoral leadership and helped them avoid fatal mistakes. They helped them survive, and eventually thrive, in their ministries.

In the late 1990s, we spoke with many new pastors who described experiences very different from those of their elders. Quite frankly, we were disturbed by what we heard from recent seminary graduates. The young pastors talked about experiences of professional and personal isolation in their churches, and only a few reported close relationships with mentors and peers. They felt that they were alone and without help, and too many were considering dropping out of the ministry altogether. They needed support to sort out early career challenges and to resist the temptation to adopt poor leadership practices. We noticed that congregations did not play much of a role in the training and development of leadership skills of these new clergy. At the same time, congregations expected recent seminary graduates to act as seasoned veterans and to be ready to tackle tricky leadership challenges on the first days of their jobs. In listening to these stories, we realized that new pastors were not prepared to meet the expectations placed on them in the early years of their ministries.

To address these challenges, the Endowment invited a few congregations and denominational judicatories to design experimental projects that would help new pastors make successful transitions into parish ministry. We were especially interested in supporting projects that would foster mentoring relationships between new and seasoned pastors as well as the formation of friendships with colleagues. We were also eager to encourage projects that would reimagine and reinforce the role congregations play in preparing young clergy to lead effectively. Our ultimate hope was that the TiM pilot projects would encourage church leaders to pay more attention to pastors in the early years of ministry and to strengthen their support networks for clergy.

The most radical—and most promising—TiM experiments have been the pastoral residency programs. Based in teaching congregations, the residency programs draw on insights from medical education and provide recent seminary graduates with short-term immersive experiences in pastoral leadership. These congregations invite new pastors to serve two-year residencies, providing them with opportunities to engage in and practice the full range of pastoral duties under the guidance of mentoring pastors. The resident pastors gather regularly with their mentors and peers to study fundamental questions about the practice of ministry and to reflect on their own leadership experiences. Congregational lay leaders also play key roles, providing support and giving the residents feedback about the effectiveness of their leadership. These churches report that these pastoral residency programs have helped them deepen their sense of mission and given new energy to their ministries.

In the pages that follow, Dr. George Mason from Wilshire Baptist Church in Dallas, Texas, provides a rich and thorough description of the pastoral residency model, exploring the demands that they place on host congregations as well as the many rich rewards they produce. Led by Dr. Mason, Wilshire has played a key role in the development and refinement of the pastoral residency model.

Reversing the recent trend, the pastoral residency programs, as you will discover in the following pages, place congregations at the center of efforts to help new ministers become effective pastoral leaders. They also demonstrate the need to foster partnerships among seminaries, congregations, and other religious organizations in order to prepare clergy for the demands of congregational leadership. Seminary classrooms are indispensable and provide settings for students to study the Bible and theology and ground themselves in the wisdom of the Christian tradition. But new pastors must learn how to draw on the wisdom of their traditions and to apply this knowledge to everyday pastoral situations. This happens best when new pastors are fully immersed in the demands of congregational leadership and engaged in ongoing reflective conversations with trusted mentors and colleagues. The pastoral residency programs provide just such settings for these immersive leadership development experiences.

Since 1999, several variations of the pastoral residency model have emerged. In its most basic form, a single congregation invites several recent seminary graduates to serve together as a residency cohort; the residents work through six-month rotations in various areas of parish life and meet weekly for study and reflection. A second variation involves a cluster of three to five congregations; working collaboratively, each congregation invites a single new pastor to serve as its resident, and all of the residents, as well as mentoring pastors, gather regularly to study and reflect on their leadership experiences. In a third variation, a judicatory office or a seminary serves as the hub for the residency program, supporting a group of congregations that each call a single new pastor to serve on its staff as a resident; the judicatory or seminary organizes and hosts the regular meetings for the new clergy. Additional variations will be described in the pages that follow.

Today, more than 152 religious organizations have participated in TiM experimental projects, including 100 congregations that invited recent seminary graduates to serve as resident pastors. The new pastors have credited their residency experiences with helping them develop healthy leadership practices, build friendships with mentors and colleagues, and establish the spiritual disciplines needed to sustain their energies over time. We have watched these projects take root and flourish, and we are delighted that these experiments have helped scores of new pastors thrive in their ministries.

We also know that we are not the only ones watching the TiM pastoral residency programs. During the last several months, we have fielded dozens of calls from pastors and congregational lay leaders who are committed to supporting new clergy and interested in establishing pastoral residency programs in their congregations. These leaders recognize the importance of helping new clergy get off to excellent starts and are prepared to take on the demands of these efforts. Yet they seek the "know how" generated by the TiM projects to address key challenges and to design high quality residency experiences.

If you are among this group, this excellent book is for you. You will find many stories and insights about the opportunities and challenges encountered by the congregations that have established outstanding pastoral residency programs. More importantly, you will find questions that your church will need to work through in order to design a residency program that is appropriate for your community. This guide presents an indispensable roadmap that will help you make wise choices and avoid costly mistakes as you explore how best to work with new pastors.

We hope that this book will stir your imagination and give you the encouragement you need to establish a pastoral residency program and become part of a growing network of congregations committed to helping new pastors get off to excellent starts in their ministries. We believe that the time is right for congregations to reclaim their role in preparing a new generation of pastoral leaders.

Christopher Coble
Program Director, Religion
Lilly Endowment Inc.

Acknowledgements

This is a book about the merits of reflective practice in the preparing of ministers for a lifetime of effective service. I have been surprised in the process of writing it by what a reflective practice the writing of it for others has been in shaping my own ministry. I hope to be a better pastor myself because of it.

If I am a better pastor, though, it will be due less to the labor of writing than to another key theme of this work—the role of the congregation. I am indebted to the Wilshire Baptist Church in Dallas, Texas, a church that models what it means to be a teaching congregation. The Wilshire people have taught me for nearly twenty-three years, and what I have learned from them is only partly summarized in these pages. I am a better pastor and a better Christian because of their extraordinary love and faithfulness. I can only hope they would testify to the feeling being mutual. I specifically want to thank Pagett Gosslee for her personal friendship and unwavering belief in this work since the beginning. She has given able lay leadership to the program for more than a decade, the last few years with the help of the Pathways to Ministry Committee and the assistance of Gladys Kolenovsky. Pathways administrator, Geri McKenzie, and my administrative assistant, Debby Burton, have run the ground game while I have operated the air attack in this mission. They have been indispensible partners day by day. My pastoral colleagues on the ministry staff—in particular Preston Bright, Mark Wingfield, Doug Haney, and Paul Johnson—have made our Pathways program into the reflexive learning community that it is. All the current and former residents of the Wilshire program have contributed to this project and to my life in ways that words cannot describe. My thanks particularly to Andrew Daugherty, Jake Hall, and Anne Jernberg for reading drafts and offering comments. Lawanna McIver Fields has been a faithful cheerleader from the moment of the program's conception, always honoring her late husband's legacy and loving her church even from afar. Steve Brookshire and Bob Coleman have been reliable friends and visionary leaders, who have also planted the seeds for future support from the congregation.

The visionary leadership of the Lilly Endowment has created the conditions that make this resource both possible and necessary. Craig Dyksta and Chris Coble have spawned a movement. The Religion Division funded a select group of pastoral residency programs in churches for more than a decade across numerous denominations. What we have learned is partly reported in these pages. The larger goal, however, is to expand this transition into ministry model to many more churches that cannot be funded through Lilly grants. This book aims to aid churches that wish to engage this mentoring endeavor on their own. My thanks especially to Chris Coble for guiding this work and carefully reading it with a view to achieving its purpose. Chris's support and encouragement along the way kept the project moving forward.

David Wood has been a friend and conversation partner from the beginning of my involvement in residency work. He oversaw the work for the Endowment through The Fund for Theological Education (FTE) before returning to the pastorate himself. Much of what came to pass in the Transition into Ministry (TiM) grant program was first hatched in David's mind as he imagined ways for churches to bridge the gaps in training ministers after seminary. He also pushed me to find my own voice in the writing. I am grateful for the subsequent leadership of Laura Cheifetz at FTE, along with the generative insights and inspiration of Melissa Wiginton, now with Education Beyond the Walls at Austin Seminary.

My colleagues and peers in TiM work consistently produce outstanding young pastors through their work. The stewardship of their ministry through mentoring gives me enormous hope for the church in the next generation. Some like Lewis Galloway, Carol Pinkham Oak, Martin Copenhaver, Chris Braudaway-Bauman, Craig Townsend, Peter Marty, and David Ruhe have been most helpful along the way. Gary Simpson's friendship has been more like brotherhood, literally.

I am grateful for my editor, Richard Bass, who smoothed out my tortured prose and tamed my penchant for long introductory clauses. His organizational wisdom in the book's development remains out of sight but not out of my mind. The Alban Institute has pioneered church consulting and publishing in a way that many have tried to copy with less success. Jim Wind's leadership of Alban continues to promote health and growth in churches all across America. I am thankful for Alban's publishing of this work and for the privilege of serving on its Board of Trustees.

Finally, my family makes ministry gratifying by understanding that the privileges we enjoy in serving the church far outweigh the responsibilities. My ageless and guileless wife, Kim, urges me on my way to preach every Sunday to "give 'em heaven." I can't imagine doing otherwise, as I can't imagine doing much worthwhile without her. My grown young adult children, Cameron, Rhett, and Jillian, have proven that healthy faith comes from healthy churches and families. "May you be so blessed yourselves."

Introduction

Congregations and Clergy Training

What kind of church will we hand over to our children and grandchildren? The answer will largely depend upon the kind of leaders we train for the church in our time. And chief among those leaders are the pastors who will serve and guide our churches.

This book reports on a new development in the training of pastors and how churches are finding new life in taking up the task. Churches are beginning to reclaim their rightful role in the formation of the ministers that will serve them. And they are learning as they do that they themselves are becoming healthier and more effective churches.

New developments come about to address crises that arise. One such crisis has been the experience of young ministers within their first five years in the parish after leaving seminary. Loneliness often accompanies a young minister who is either a solo pastor in a church or much younger than other staff. Feelings of inadequacy and frustration with the church can emerge from criticism of lay people that may or may not be warranted. Congregational ministry demands a level of

1

skill that seminaries cannot adequately refine, and such areas as finances, budgets, personnel management, and vocational identity are also not well suited to seminary study. Faced with these challenges, some young ministers begin to question their call, and too many drop out of ministry altogether.

Everyone—from the church to the seminary to the minister himself—has a vested interest in helping young pastors get off to a good start. The foundation for a lifetime of ministry is laid in the first few years, for good or ill. Making this time spiritually generative and vocationally healthy is what this book seeks to address.

Among the new ways churches are taking up this work is through the creation of pastoral residency programs: a congregation invites one or more young ministers to join the pastoral staff for two or three years, and then the church sends them out to their first full-time call in another congregation. Pastoral residency provides a period of transition during which seminary graduates can begin the work of ministry under the supervision of an experienced pastoral team, with the support of key lay leaders and the collegiality of peers.

The residency period allows young ministers the opportunity to hone such skills as preaching, teaching, pastoral care, and administration in a nurturing culture that will strengthen the young minister's confidence and competence in serving the church. Residents are treated as pastors, albeit fledgling ones. The church helps them to accept the pastoral life and the habits of ministry that make it up.

These are interesting times for the church. The oft-heard cry that the church is dying, evidenced by membership and attendance declines in some quarters, fails to account for the resilient hope Christians live by. The church is Christ's body, and Christ's body is ever dying and rising again. We only have to widen our vision or shift our gaze to see signs of new life in the church. Protestant and Pentecostal churches to the south and east—that is, in Central and South America, in Africa, and in South Korea and China, for instance—are much chronicled for their gains in number and vitality. The entrepreneurial emerging church movement in North America taps into the hunger for relevance and authenticity many young people experience, adapting to and adopting the more casual and technologically savvy lifestyle that is reshaping daily life.

Signs of new life are appearing also among more traditional Mainline Protestant and Catholic churches that remain committed to carrying forward and passing on ancient practices, tested liturgy, and sturdy structures for communal faith. Churches like these play their own important role in the larger body of Christ. While some churches innovate by focusing on particular theological approaches, targeted demographic strategies, or contemporary worship styles to reach people otherwise uncommitted or uninvolved, established churches are designed for the ages—all ages, that is, and from age to age.

All churches know things they don't even know they know— things that have been passed on to them and that they can pass on to the next generation—if only they will become aware enough of what they know in order to teach it. Our churches need to teach what we know to those who will teach others as we have taught them. Wisdom resides in pew and pulpit alike. Clergy and laity are important to this work of training leaders for the church from generation to generation.

This book may be used as a resource for churches and pastors who want to engage in this work. It is designed especially for churches that want to create and sustain mentoring programs for young pastors in their transition from seminary or divinity school to congregational ministry.

Successful clergy training programs require teaching congregations that will become, at the same time, learning communities of shared reflective practices.[1] Teaching congregations take a special interest in communicating the whys and wherefores, as well as the how and how-comes, to those who do the work of ministry. Pastors pastor, but at the same time they help young ministers become pastors, too. Laypersons don't just listen to sermons and teach preschoolers and serve in the food pantry; they say what they are hearing to those who are preaching, they bring others alongside them as they teach and show them how to do it, and they help others catch a vision for mission by encouraging their service. Teaching congregations adapt. They learn from what they do and become better at it either by repetition or by changing their approach. But teaching congregations have a special interest in passing on the church to the next generation. One slice of that concern—the training of tomorrow's clergy—is where pastoral residency comes in.

As the church sets out to do one thing—train effective clergy—it will discover a surprising byproduct: it will become more alive on both sides of the Communion rail. What's more, it will become more effective at training lay leaders. Like a spider web, touch it at any place and it will affect every other place on the web.

Gifted and capable leaders—clergy and lay both—give churches energy and direction. Each depends upon the other in the work of building strong churches for their own time and place and for the work of the church beyond their time and in other places.

⁓

Over the last decade a few dozen churches, employing various models unique to their own church cultures, have been pioneering and experimenting with the practice of training clergy. Other models sponsored by denominations or local judicatories have used congregations in different but similar ways to foster better transitions into ministry for young clergy. Some of their stories will be told here as a way of encouraging others to undertake this work.

These programs have shaped the young ministers being trained and at the same time renewed the churches doing the training. In the process of mentoring the young ministers, senior pastors, permanent staff, and key lay leaders have found new joy in their own ministries. While this work takes place in local churches and energizes those churches in the process, its larger effect on the wider church is only now beginning to be seen, as these well-formed young pastors find their places in the congregations that call them to serve.

Partnership of Church and School

But why should a church engage in this work? Isn't it the job of seminaries and divinity schools to prepare ministers for our churches? Yes and no. Theological schools do their part in training ministers, but they are not the only agent in the process. Churches also have a crucial role to play. Likewise, churches are not only the beneficiaries of theological education; they are bearers of spiritual wisdom that must be conveyed to would-be clergy. Clergy training requires a robust partnership between the academy and the congregation. Neither can do alone what needs to be done. And it's the nature of the learning that needs to be done that makes this clear.

Daniel Aleshire, who oversees the accrediting body of theological schools in North America, makes the case that schools and churches provide two different kinds of learning environments, both of which are essential to gaining knowledge and wisdom for pastoral work. "Schools are absolutely superb at certain kinds of learning," he says. "If you want to exegete the Greek text [of the New Testament], go to school, take baby Greek, then take intermediate Greek, then exegetical courses. If you pay attention and learn your lessons, you will be able to exegete a Greek text. If you want to learn the history of the church, go to school, take a course on early Christian origins and the New Testament, then Patristics, then church history prior to the Reformation, then church history post Reformation, and top it off with a history of your part of the Christian family. If you have studied your lessons, you will know a great deal about church history at the end of your school experience."[2]

We want our pastors to know these things. We want our doctors to know anatomy, chemistry, and the history of surgery. We want our lawyers to know the Constitution, legal procedure, and the history of jurisprudence. In like manner we want our pastors to know the grammar of faith, our foundational texts and how to interpret them, and the history of the church in all its various shapes.

But knowing these things, and even being able to teach these things to others, does not make for an able pastor. Another kind of learning is needed, too, and it's a kind of learning that can only take place in the midst of the practice of ministry in a congregational setting, where such ministry most often takes place.

When I reflect upon my own ministerial training, I am grateful for the theological inheritance that was passed on to me by the seminary I attended. My training in biblical interpretation, theology, and church history gave me more than my own biases to test in pastoral practice. Seminary training gave me the witness of the church across time to take with me into my time of church ministry.

Seminary education leans more toward information than formation. It makes deposits of biblical and theological knowledge in the bank account of a young minister that she will be able to draw upon throughout her ministry. Seminary can only gesture toward the pastoral life, however, because the school classroom favors a learning mode germane to its purpose, while the church setting makes possible a different kind of learning that grows out of doing ministry itself.

It's not so simple as to say that theory precedes practice, though, since theory and practice shape each other in the continual conversation between the church and the academy. Good seminary training and good congregational practice mutually reinforce one another. Those who dismiss seminary education as unimportant to ministry training miss a key component in the process.

And yet, the deficit in training among those who are seminary educated is often found more in the direction of the congregation. I was five years into pastoral work when I heard a chaplain in a hospital room tell a family about their options for a deceased loved one's services, distinguishing between a funeral and a memorial service. It was embarrassing to realize that I could talk about matters of the soul's eternal destiny with relative competence, but I couldn't describe with proper terminology the differences of how the body would be treated in Christian services for the dead. Furthermore, I was well into my second pastorate before I understood the significance of the words of institution for the Lord's Supper. For churches that use a book of worship, the prescribed words are there in black and white to be recited. But those of us who serve in less formal liturgical contexts are expected to speak words over the elements that interpret the meal as something holy in the partaking of it together. These words may or may not have sacramental import (a long debated theological point), but they at least point the communicants to the spiritual nature of the meal, the biblical link to Christ, and the historic connection to the church across time. Yet I had no instruction in crafting these words at the Table.

How I could have missed these things in my training is puzzling, but perhaps the fault is not so much in the curriculum of the seminary as in the locus of the training. The Rev. Jim Gertmenian has memories of similar inadequacy in his first church out of seminary. He found himself faced with conducting a funeral for the first time, and he realized he had only attended two funerals in his lifetime. Now the senior pastor at Plymouth Congregational Church, a 2,100 member congregation in Minneapolis that conducts a pastoral residency program, Gertmenian doesn't blame the seminary for his early ministry gap in pastoral skill. "I have tremendous respect for what seminaries do," he says, "but for all their good efforts, they aren't able to replicate the range of situations that prepare students for the 'daily-ness' of parish ministry. There are certain skills that a pastor acquires only by working in a church setting."[3]

Some things are better caught than taught. But they aren't best caught by osmosis—just by being in the same setting where others do these things. They are caught by doing them together with others in a congregational setting and then reflecting upon the doing of them with experienced practitioners.

Churches do ministry. They are communities of shared practices. Sunday worship, for instance, isn't just about a preacher who prepares and delivers a sermon. It's also about the congregation that hears the sermon, the sound technician who aids them in the hearing, the young acolyte who lights the candles, the choir that sings, the organist who accompanies, the secretary who types and reproduces the order of service, and the custodian who cleans the pews and checks the room temperature. And those are just the more obvious participants. We could also count those across the ages who wrote, translated, and preserved the Bible we read. Or those who labored to give us the denomination we serve in and the particular local church we worship in on any given Sunday. Multiply this instance by the many acts of hospitality, pastoral care, religious education, benevolence, and justice work, and you see that every aspect of ministry involves many partners. Which also means that effective pastoral training is hardly an individual learning endeavor; it truly is a group effort.

This is what pastoral residency work is about. Residents begin to get a feel for the pastoral role and for the nuances of ministry. They perform all the duties of the pastorate, albeit under the guidance of a mentor pastor and within a supportive and engaging community of faith. This extends their training and enhances their readiness to serve in permanent pastoral positions in their next churches.

Seminaries and congregations working in partnership with one another, respecting the unique domains for learning that each provides, will round out the pastor's formation in ways that will make the transition into full-time vocational ministry more fulfilling and likely more successful.

Perhaps the key distinction between the two domains of school and church is that the former is more preparatory, the latter more participatory. Seminaries can teach you things that will help you do ministry when you get there, but residencies involve the doing of those things when you are already there. As one resident put it: "This isn't a classroom; it's the real thing."[4] Said another way, good pastoral learning involves both experience and reflection. Seminaries specialize in reflection without being able to provide the setting of experience. Churches complete the cycle by being places of experience.

And yet, experience alone is not enough. Experience can be good or bad; the more important thing is how it shapes the character of the pastor going forward. Experience can discourage growth, distort call, and degrade confidence as surely as it can encourage, clarify, and improve a young minister's knowledge and practice. Pastoral residency allows opportunities for thoughtful reflection on all of these ministry experiences in a safe environment, and the ability to be reflective about one's experience is a more important indicator of what kind of pastor one will become than the actual experiences themselves. Residents learn from things done well and begin to ingrain these into their ministry skill set. They learn too from mistakes that they will be less likely to repeat when they serve in their next churches.

Effective church-based pastoral education is reflective experience in which residents practice ministry in a collaborative environment that includes both clergy and laypersons. Residents do and discuss, discuss and do; and at each stage of the process they are honing their competence and growing in confidence.[5]

Pastoral residency programs are a laboratory and a launching pad for the ministers that will one day serve our churches. We want them to be the best they can be, and getting off to a good start is crucial to their long-term leadership success and satisfaction in ministry.

Distinguishing Residencies from Other Mentoring

Church members will have to learn terminology as you begin a clergy residency program. Over and again you will hear residents called interns, because internship is a more widely shared term within various fields. Interns are found in education, business, medicine, law, and social work, to name a few. Churches also host internship programs to great benefit. But for the purpose of this work, we make a distinction between internships and residencies.

Churches often recruit college students who wish to explore ministry as a vocation to serve as full-time summer interns or part-time semester interns. These young people help permanent staff with children and youth programs, such as camps, Bible schools, and community mission work. They add manpower, and they strengthen programs at little or no cost. The church benefits from the intern's time and effort, and the intern benefits by getting a taste for ministry. This experience leads the intern one more step in the discernment process of call to ministry.

Churches that pay attention to nurturing the call of young people into ministry will want to employ internships as part of that process. The Fund for Theological Education (FTE) has done extensive work with congregations that engage in what they have called the three-step approach of Notice, Name, and Nurture.[6] FTE has also researched best practices of congregations that provide internships for young people. Mentoring interns involves allowing them to test the waters, so to speak, without diving in. It will help them to sense whether they want to wade deeper into ministry discernment. By contrast, residency is an immersion experience, with the added benefit of a lifeguard on duty at all times.

But before we describe residential immersion more fully, two other kinds of internships should be distinguished from residencies: hospital-based Clinical Pastoral Education (CPE) and church-based seminary field education. CPE programs are sometimes included in pastoral training as a means of preparing ministers for one key aspect of their work in the care of souls. These programs introduce young ministers to a rigorous process of self-examination that makes them aware of how their own story affects the way they interact with persons dealing with physical or emotional illness. They teach, in a clinical setting, how to listen and respond to individuals, families, and caregivers, adding a spiritual component to the healing process. Hospital chaplaincy departments generally conduct these programs under the accrediting auspices of the Association for Clinical Pastoral Education. They call the ministers interns during their initial units of this kind of pastoral training. Aside from the hospital setting, the other difference from church-based residencies is that the pastoral care in CPE programs tends toward acute or critical care episodes, while church-based residencies train pastors in dealing with parishioners in the ongoing continuum of wellness and illness—both acute and chronic—within the life cycle of individuals, families, and the congregation.

Seminary field education programs come closer to church-based residencies but still fall short of what is entailed in the latter. Field education closes the gap between the academy and the church.[7] The school enlists willing churches to receive seminarians and expose them to ministry in a congregational setting. Most churches are expected to provide the student with a stipend and a mentor. Program expectations vary from school to school, as does the duration of the internship: some are summer experiences, some one semester or two, and some are a year in length.

Most schools will guide the student through the internship by making sure the church and mentor are trained and accountable to the school for what is learned. Students pay the school and are graded by the school during their internships. Ironically, the fact that the school sets the standards and does the training for field education runs counter to the point of it. Whom you are accountable to determines where your attention will lie. Moreover, schools tend to measure education by the mastery of knowledge rather than skill. And skill is both harder to measure and better judged by practitioners in the congregational setting.

Field education internships lead students into a deeper engagement with congregational ministry and, therefore, a more informed discernment process. But as Jocelyn Emerson, a former pastoral resident at Hyde Park Union Church in Chicago, put it, "Field education doesn't give you the total pastoral experience. You don't get to meet with the church board and learn how budgeting works." Residents, on the other hand, learn administration, Christian education, urban outreach, pastoral care, and preaching while *doing* them. By the time they complete their residencies, they will have performed weddings and funerals and baptisms, planned and led worship, delivered sermons, moderated staff and committee meetings, and coordinated mission activities. "The residency program made me a pastor at Hyde Park Union Church," says Emerson, "and with that comes all the stuff of the church."

Churches that conduct pastoral residency programs declare a pastor a pastor in order to make her a pastor. In other words, young ministers adopt a new identity—a pastoral identity. And that can only happen after the robe is donned.

Congregations play a crucial part in this formation of pastoral identity. They confer the role in order for the identity to be confirmed. They allow a young minister to move from knowing himself as one who is called to be a pastor to one who is called Pastor. Too many pastors never feel settled into their role or comfortable answering to their title. They feel somehow fraudulent to be called Pastor, because they assume they have to be a finished product in order to earn the role. Congregations form pastoral identity into young ministers partly by loving them into the role, entrusting themselves to the care of the would-be pastor, and in doing so undermine the myth of pastoral perfection that would otherwise sabotage a minister's future. This builds humility and grace into a developing pastor because of the grace and trust granted by the church.

But churches don't grant such grace and trust indiscriminately. They expect a certain readiness and training as prerequisite to pastoral practice. Residents have the requisite training. Returning to the metaphor of the clerical robe, interns try on the vestments of ministry; residents wear them. This distinction makes all the difference for learning. Interns are students discerning whether to become pastors. Residents are pastors learning to be pastors.

Pastoral residency is similar to medical residency. Like medical residents, pastoral residents have completed their classroom work. They have graduated from professional schools and have been admitted to the collegial body of trained practitioners. Nevertheless, in their early years of practice, they benefit by doing their work under the mentoring gaze of a seasoned colleague.

Tasha Gibson, a pastoral resident alumna from Wilshire Baptist Church in Dallas, uses the analogy of family to describe another dimension of the impact of residencies as compared to internships. "An intern is welcomed into the church family for a short time to observe and learn from that family. The resident is invited into the family and is given permission to be a part of the family. Being a part of the family alters the family dynamics, changing the way the family relates within itself and to others. Internships, partly because of time span and partly because of their exploratory nature, do not allow for the same degree of closeness and engagement in a local congregation. Residencies offer the space and time for young pastors to more deeply connect to members of the congregation and to the life of the community—which ends up changing both of them." Residencies have a level of mutuality that internships lack. Everyone is able to grow in the relationship because of the design of the program and the openness of all parties.

How to Use This Resource

Churches that want to consider whether to begin a pastoral residency program will profit from the knowledge and experience gained by those churches that have already ventured into this work. This book will attempt to lead key clergy and lay leaders in a church through the important factors that go into a successful program, and at the same time it will highlight areas to watch out for that may undermine the undertaking. It's hoped that senior pastors and congregational leaders will read this together in the decision-making process. Every question will not be answered, but every attempt will be made to describe the crucial components of a pastoral residency program.

The residency programs that have modeled this work over the last decade have produced helpful materials, some of which can be found on the Transition into Ministry website at www.fteleaders.org/pages/TiM. This site also lists the contact information for churches and denominational programs that have engaged in this work.

Any church that begins a pastoral residency program will be able to learn from others that have already done it, but each church will also shape its program in ways that are unique to the culture and context of that congregation. Which means that this resource can only do so much; the rest will be left to prayer and discernment within and among the leaders of the churches themselves.

Chapter 1

Assessing Readiness

Discerning Whether to Launch a Residency Program

"Look before you leap," the old saying goes. That's good advice for any congregation considering whether to launch a pastoral residency program.

A successful residency program enriches the life of a church and strengthens the broader Church at the same time. A successful one, that is. An unsuccessful program can scar the young ministers who participate in it and mar the church that fails to live up to the hopes it had for it. As in any venture, the presence of certain assets to begin with will increase the likelihood of success. The absence of these should give the church pause about whether to proceed.

A Teaching Congregation

The question before "to do or not to do" a residency program is Shakespearean: "to be or not to be" a teaching congregation? A teaching congregation is a learning community in which ministry is performed *and* continuously examined. It's a culture of shared reflective practices, a way of being more than a way of doing.

The medical model serves as a point of comparison. Some hospitals focus solely on patient care; others are teaching hospitals that include the training of doctors, nurses, and other caregivers in the process of doing patient care. Teaching hospitals provide opportunities for young professionals to practice their healing art under the watchful eye of more experienced practitioners. Instead of having the possible effect of lowering the quality of patient care, the culture of learning creates higher quality care in both young and experienced caregivers. Iron sharpens iron, as the proverb says. But in order for that to happen, patients must be willing to have less experienced doctors and other medical personnel attend to them, supervising practitioners must be generous with their time and attention to those who are learning by their side, and hospitals must make deliberate attempts to structure their caregiving in this educational model.

Some churches have long functioned with a pastoral staff that provides ministry to the congregation, looking after the needs of the laity, performing worship, and teaching adult Bible studies as trained religious professionals. Parishioners in these churches see themselves as consumers more than contributors. They receive ministry rather than perform it. Ministry is delegated to the professionals. The staff serves the church that receives its ministry more than shares in it. The staff also represents the church in its ministry to the community.

While we can debate whether any church should function that way, we have to be honest enough to admit that some do. These churches are not good candidates for pastoral residency programs because they will only serve to perpetuate a model of ministry that focuses on what can be done now instead of what can be learned for the future. A pastoral residency program would be an alien intrusion into a reigning church culture that features a style of "ministry *to*" rather than "ministry *with*" the people. It would require a deliberate and conscious attempt to change the culture in the process of instituting a program. Additionally, if a church is not used to asking the "Why" question about what it does, a residency program that by its nature asks about the ways and means of everything a church does will seem to bring criticism to a culture that isn't used to it and might not welcome it as constructive. On the contrary, a church that can point to learning practices already resident within its history has a better chance of deepening those practices with a residency program than one that would have to create a learning culture first.

Sometimes the roots for this are already present in the church's story and may be named and reclaimed without a complete overhaul in the ministry model. For example, in my own church the language of teaching congregation was certainly not pew parlance. But my predecessor as senior pastor had been a key figure fifty years earlier in the youth revival movement that swept the South after World War II and had written a book about its effects in calling out a new generation of Baptist ministers.[1]

The Rev. Bruce McIver had served Wilshire Baptist Church for thirty years prior to my tenure, and then another twelve years as pastor emeritus before his death. The relationship between us was mutually supportive and affectionate. Although there was no formal mentoring component to the relationship, many thought of it in those terms and saw it as an unusually healthy model of transition from an older to a younger pastor.

We were able, therefore, to remind the church during the readiness assessment process that this is who we are and have been. We were able to point to numerous examples of formal and informal internship efforts with young and aspiring ministers, to relationships with seminaries, and to financial support of theological education. A pastoral residency program became a way for us to fertilize the seeds that were already organically planted in the soil of the church's history.

Similarly, the Charles Street African Methodist Episcopal Church in Boston, like many historically black churches in America, has a long history of informal mentoring of young ministers. Since 2001, Charles Street Church has hosted a pastoral residency program under the leadership of senior pastor Greg Groover, but it has a rich tradition of nurturing young ministers and sending them on to school for theological training. One resident was a third-generation minister to be trained in some fashion by the church.

A church that already places a high value on education may raise this to a more conscious level. Many churches—whether the pews are filled with formally educated people or not—are passionate about seeing young people ascend toward higher learning. They especially value an educated clergy, often, as with the Charles Street Church, having sponsored promising young people through seminary or divinity school. Pastoral residency work extends this educational interest into a formative one.

Churches that habitually send ministerial students away to be educated are welcoming them (whether their own or other young people) back to finish that education in the church setting. Although the distinction is not absolute, one way of putting this is to say that church education of residents is formative, while seminary education is informative. Church-based education majors in the practical wisdom of pastoral work after the seminary has supplied the necessary knowledge of the faith. The larger point, however, is that a church with a tradition of educating young ministers will be ripe for pastoral residency work.

The presence of teachers and educational administrators in the congregation will also help. Other professionals, such as doctors, lawyers, and accountants, who experience mentoring relationships in their daily work may contribute to strengthening this identity. Having a supply of professional people in the church who are familiar with professional mentoring of any kind will aid in the development of a program.

A pastoral staff that constantly asks itself questions about its ministry—how to grow in effectiveness, how to work together as a team, and how to nurture lay leadership—will be crucial. They will be an example of a learning community for young ministers and also for lay people. But the presence of good lay leadership cannot be overstated. Lay people may also model reflective practice for young ministers.

Pastoral residents who report on their experience often cite lay leaders as great teachers. One resident, Jake Caldwell, of Central Christian Church in Lexington, Kentucky, tells of gaining valuable insights about church finances and governance from lay leaders who took time with him. One example illustrates: "Following a board meeting in which there was contentious debate about the role of the administrative board in hiring and firing a minister, one of the older members took me aside and told me about several instances in which the dismissal of ministers had been a divisive event in the life of the church. Some of these stories dated back at least sixty years, yet a number of people who were involved back then are still active in the church. They were bringing a history that I did not know about into our discussion. It was a history I needed to understand what was happening." Other residents tell similar stories. They consistently mention patience and deliberation as values lay leaders have taught them.

Lay leaders who generously take time with residents to guide them through the subtleties of church culture and polity are treasures to developing ministers. Their presence in a congregation makes a pastoral residency program doable. One pastor says it this way: "Without key lay people, a church can't imagine doing a pastoral residency program. With them, it can't imagine not doing it."

The setting of the church can also provide strong rationale for taking the step into pastoral residency work. The Rev. Peter C. Lane, rector of St. Paul & the Redeemer Episcopal Church (SPR) in the Hyde Park community of Chicago, notes how the church's location influenced its decision to initiate a residency program. The calling to raise up leadership, he says, "flows out of the culture of our neighborhood, the proximity of so many seminaries, and particular human resources in the parish. Hyde Park is a training ground; people come to Hyde Park to learn how to do something well. That spirit infuses the culture of SPR to the point where it is nearly assumed that everyone is developing himself or herself." Lane points to the six seminaries located nearby and a rich array of congregational leaders—lay and ordained—who are committed to leadership development.

In sum, a congregation that is ready to take the next step in launching a pastoral residency program will contain precedents in its own history or elements in its environment that may make the decision to do this work seem a natural extension of work already going on. At best it may feel like a spiritual mandate.

A Healthy Church

"Churches are either plums or pills," an older colleague once declared to me as I was discerning whether to accept a call to a certain congregation. "Make sure this one is a plum." It would have been easier to figure out if he hadn't mixed his metaphors, if I could have devised one taste test or blind study to determine a plum or a pill. Another experienced pastor was more helpful: "Churches have either problem-making or problem-solving cultures." Healthy churches find ways to address the challenges they face without degenerating into toxic conflict. They build confidence over time that they have the spiritual and relational resources necessary to make the community of Christ a witness to the promise of new creation and not a lingering sign of the sin and sickness of a world passing away.

Healthy congregations ought to reproduce themselves. We want their kind to propagate. Unhealthy congregations can get healthy, but they certainly should not expect a pastoral residency program to cure what ails them. That would be like a married couple deciding to have children as a way of resolving conflict between them. The effect of that will more likely be that they will teach another generation to repeat the same mistakes they have made.

Churches that host pastoral residency programs have a formative effect on young ministers in the way those future pastors come to view the church as well as how they develop their skills in serving it. If the church they train in is a healthy congregation, it will instill a vision of vitality and sound functioning in the novice pastor that will remain for years to come.

When Wilshire Baptist Church was discussing whether to call me as pastor in 1989, a line of questioning arose about my youth and inexperience during a congregational meeting. "Is he up to the challenge of leading a large church like ours?" they asked. After some back and forth about my age and maturity, about whether I could grow into the job, and so forth, an elderly deacon rose to speak from the back of the room. "It seems to me that we are putting the question the wrong way. It's not a matter of whether he's up to the challenge; it's whether we are. Great pastors don't make great churches," he said. "Great churches make great pastors."

Conversely, churches that find themselves in perpetual conflict have a way of taking the heart out of a pastor. Pastoral ministry is challenging to begin with. It requires sacrifices small and large. Pastors have to persevere. They shouldn't expect congregational Camelot, given that even a church founded by Christ and animated by his Spirit is a human institution. But like families that fall on a continuum between functional and dysfunctional, pastoral residency work is most successful in a church that is more life-giving than life-draining.

How then do you determine whether your church is healthy enough to move further down the road of discernment toward initiating a residency program? Many have attempted to assign markers to what constitutes a healthy church. These attempts generally reflect the theological or denominational tradition in which the expert has been formed. Or perhaps the definitions of health are sociological and financial. But is a church that is growing numerically and monetarily automatically a healthy church? Or course not. They may have fleeting appeal. Healthy churches are deep and wide both. They have spiritual depth and increasing scope.

The more important question of congregational health may be whether it experiences itself as a spiritual community of well-being. Two questions for congregational reflection to that end may be:

1. *Does the church have a long record of holding together through times of dispute, or have church splits been the key to ever-narrowing unity?* People will come and go in every church. Conflict increases the likelihood that people will leave the membership. Sometimes people will join the church after that time, partly due to a clearer congregational identity. But if the church has a history of splitting, it would not possess important resources to share with a novice pastor about how to help a congregation work through its challenges and stay together. Stability is a bedrock virtue of a congregation that is ready to begin a residency program.

2. *Is there evidence that the church has an adventurous spirit that can try new things?* If the virtue of stability keeps a church grounded, creativity defies gravity. Churches need this kind of tension between being security minded, which assures continuity, and risk-taking, which adds vitality and opens the church to new possibilities. Every venture does not have to succeed in order

to be successful. Because the church is not a business per se, it doesn't have to show a financial return on investment in order to justify a new ministry. Because the church is the body of Christ that is ever dying and rising again, it can risk itself for the sake of the gospel and find that the very venture undertaken that looks to some like failure may in fact have transformed the lives of those involved, making it successful in spiritual ways. But if a church has no history of risking failure by attempting new things, it will have a hard time creating a pastoral residency program that will demand much of the congregation.

Healthy churches are congregations that keep stability and creativity in tension. They hold together the tried and true with the untried and new. They imagine what may be without neglecting what has been. They exercise prudence and faith at the same time.

A Pastor Who Loves the Work

Another key factor in discerning whether to start a residency program concerns the senior pastor of the church. This should be obvious. You wouldn't consider training a blacksmith without an experienced smithy who loves to shoe horses, and neither would you begin a pastoral apprenticeship program without an experienced pastor who loves to serve a congregation.

This has several implications. First, a pastor should be in place and have a good relationship with the congregation. The engagement of the senior pastor in residency programs has proven to be crucial to their success. When a church tries to conduct a program without a pastor, whether because of a change in the pastoral office that leaves it vacant for a time or because the pastor delegates the work to an associate, the program is hampered. It is important to have a senior pastor on site, preferably with some tenure in that congregation and committed to the success of the residency program. An effective residency program can't be built exclusively on the senior pastor, but it can't be built well without a good one.

Second, churches are best prepared to begin such a venture when they have a pastor with a proven track record of service. Young ministers learn best when their mentors have a reservoir of experience to share with them. While peer learning adds greatly to the experience, the foundation of a residency model is the mentoring of an inexperienced minister by an experienced pastor.

A smithy knows when to hammer the iron, when to put it into the fire and when to let it cool, and how to get the horse still enough to affix the shoe. Similarly, apprentice pastors learn by observing, asking questions, and then doing themselves those pastoral tasks that require a kind of intangible feel. Pastors don't just preach, they preach in ways that push the congregation at times and pull at other times. Pastors remind congregants that they are accepted as they are, and pastors also call them to become all they can be. Pastors have to know when to say what. They also have to know when to lead and when to follow, when to step in administratively and when to step back.

Pastors who will serve as mentors need the benefit of learned intuition that can only be acquired in the crucible of congregational life over time. And even pastors who have much experience in ministry but little with their current congregation may struggle to pass on these insights because they may be preoccupied with establishing their own relationship to the new church. It's best for a pastoral residency program if the congregation has a pastor with some years of experience behind her, both in ministry generally and with that church particularly.

Next, the pastor needs to have a strong enough sense of self to make room for the pastoral resident in his ministry. This is more than a matter of sharing office space; it's about the soul space the mentor will make for the mentee. It has to do with being secure enough to celebrate the ministry of the younger pastor, to delight in her growth, to hear compliments from the congregation about the younger pastor without feeling threatened personally. It means generously sharing ministry opportunities and ministry struggles. Furthermore, young ministers will learn much by hearing about their mentor's failures as well as successes. But they will only hear about those if the minister is secure enough to acknowledge them and share them.

In a different field, Bruce Marantz has modeled this truth. Marantz is an accomplished jazz musician who has played in bands with such luminaries as Ray Charles. But today he teaches budding young musicians at Dallas's Booker T. Washington High School for the Performing and Visual Arts. Among his protégés are names like Norah Jones, Roy Hargrove, and Erykah Badu. Some wonder whether it feels more like the student teaching the teacher. "I've come to a point in my life," says Marantz, "where I'm OK with that. I just want to see the music carry on and go forward." His students sing his praises, even though their names have become bigger than his. A fellow jazz instructor at the school summarizes his contribution by saying that Marantz "can give the kids something that doesn't come out of books. He's definitely a contributor to the national jazz scene."[2]

Marantz's willingness to count his success as much through the success of his students as his own musicianship makes him a model mentor. And the fact that he offers something they couldn't receive by reading a book correlates to the performance character of pastoral ministry also.

This leads to another crucial component of effective senior pastor mentors: they must be turned toward this work as a central part of their ministry. They can't view residents as peripheral to their ministry, as research assistants to aid their preaching or writing, or as arrows in their vocational quiver that they can shoot into the future to extend their legacy. They must see the nurture and formation of younger pastors as an integral aspect of their work in serving Christ and his church.

David Ruhe testifies to a moment of epiphany in his life that changed the way he viewed his pastoral work. After many years of serving churches, including his current charge as the senior pastor of the Plymouth Congregational Church of Des Moines, Iowa, he found himself one day alone in his car at a stoplight. What happened next made him stop vocationally, even as it shed light on where to go next. He felt like he heard a voice speaking to him (or was it a Voice?). "Ruhe, you're not the young guy anymore. Something different is required of you now. Act your age. What the church needs from you right now is a sage." That revelation became a mission. He realized that his ministry had turned a corner and he had to turn with it.

Pastors who do this work well describe this turn different ways, but they are all clear that something has to shift in their perspective on ministry. They no longer look for satisfaction only in their own work; they begin to find it in the work of others. They see the job of passing on their knowledge and wisdom as constitutive of their daily work. They develop a new clarity that "It's not about me." They ask themselves less often "how am I doing?" and more often "how are they doing because of me?" The "they," of course, are the resident pastors in their care.

Finally, mentor pastors have to love their work and show it. What young pastors learn will be caught as much as taught. The honorable nature of the pastoral calling and the privilege of carrying it out in good times and bad must emanate from the spirit of the senior pastor. Some pastors undermine their own work by nourishing negativity in private while maintaining a positive posture in public. That divided self will frustrate young ministers and may cause them to lose their passion for the work.

Christ loved the church and gave himself up for it, Paul says in Ephesians 5. The sacrifice of giving himself up was willingly made out of love for his bride, the church. Those of us who serve churches in Christ's name must have the same kind of love, if not the same measure of it. It is rewarding work and often joyful, even when hard and challenging. This spirit will inspire the next generation of pastors to love the church and serve it with glad and generous hearts. To do so doesn't deny the difficulty of ministry so much as profess a robust confidence in God that our work will never be done in vain.

A Clear Mission

Why are we doing this? What do we expect to accomplish? A church that undertakes to conduct a pastoral residency program will not have all the answers ahead of time, but it should have appropriate intention.

Before beginning a pastoral residency program, the congregation will require education. Key leaders—both staff and lay—should give informed consent. Whatever ruling body the church employs should sign up for the challenge. The more work done ahead of time to prepare the church and to generate enthusiasm for the program the better. For those churches that operate within connectional systems, informing and gaining consent from judicatory leaders will be important.

When our church began to think about doing this work in 2001, we were serendipitously engaged in a strategic planning process. One key priority that emerged in that process was that the church would intentionally "mobilize missional servants." Within that priority, one strategy that the church adopted read this way: "Wilshire will nurture and train a new generation of Baptist ministers in a premier church-based clergy apprenticeship program." That mission statement was then approved by the congregation, along with the rest of the strategic plan, and the church had a mandate to proceed. Such a statement "languaged the future" before it came to pass.

Word-making becomes world-making, as the biblical creation demonstrates. The same is also true with the creation of new church programs like pastoral residency. The church needs to speak it into being. And the more voices that can speak it together, the greater the probability its life will be long and fruitful.

Wise pastors and keen lay leaders also know, however, that there are often informal processes that should be undertaken in churches in order to insure a successful launch of any new ministry. Sometimes that involves conversations with nonelected leaders of the congregation whom people respect because of their faithfulness across time. Sometimes it involves getting ahead of naysayers who tend to revel in criticism if they have not been personally included in the decision-making process. Sometimes it involves conversation with people of means whose support may make the difference between an adequate and a well-funded future program. Taking the time to think through and talk through the informal as well the formal processes of church life will be worth the investment. The more buy-in the church can attain from the more constituencies the better.

Adequate Financial Resources

Thus far we have talked about discerning whether to proceed based upon an asset inventory that includes an established or burgeoning learning culture among staff and laity, a healthy history of church functioning that balances stability and creativity, a pastor with experience and a passion for the church and this work, and a clearly defined mission for the program that has been endorsed by key constituents. One glaring omission is capital. How much money does it take to do this? That's the first question many churches will ask, and it's an important one. But it's not the first question, because money follows mission, not the other way round.

Whether financial support for a pastoral residency program comes from a church's budget, from special gifts, from grants by foundations, or from estate gifts by parishioners who generously planned ahead to support future generations of congregational leadership, a vision for work like this—along with the human and spiritual capital necessary to carry it out—must first be in place. A pastoral residency program can be expensive, and we'll look more closely in chapter 8 at estimates of costs and various ways of locating startup funding and then money to sustain the program. But for now, assume a God of abundance and a people of largesse. If the mission is right, it's more likely the money will be right along when the time is right.

Chapter 2

Customizing a Model

SELECTING A BLUEPRINT TO MAKE YOUR OWN

If you were planning to build a house, you would consider things like the size and configuration of the family that would live in it. You would design the floor plan to match the way the family structures its time, hobbies, and practices of hospitality. You would also look at other houses in the neighborhood in order to make sure that the style of architecture you favor adds value to the community. You might hire an architect and begin to design the house from scratch, but alternatively you might look at model homes that you could customize. With a model blueprint in front of you, you could change certain aspects of the design without radically revising the house plan. This would save money and worry, since some version of the plan will have been used previously and has, therefore, been tested.

Similarly, if you determine to move forward with a pastoral residency program for your church, you could start fresh with your own ideas and create your own model. You could be your own architect and design the program from scratch. Chances are, though, that what you come up with will look a lot like what has already been tried. You will save a fair amount of time and effort, maybe even cost—and certainly reduce your punch list—by selecting a model that you can then customize for your own church.

When we began the Wilshire residency program, we didn't know that anyone else was already engaged in this work. We began to sketch out a design for one pastoral resident, but didn't know many things yet about the optimum duration of the program, relation to permanent staff, what reflective practices would best serve the formation of a pastor, how much lay involvement would be helpful, or how much it would cost. In the months leading up to our program launch, I read an article in the Alban Institute's magazine *Congregations* (April 2002), which told of the Lilly Endowment's effort to address the challenges of the transition into ministry faced by young pastors. The article especially focused on the pilot effort of the Second Presbyterian Church of Indianapolis, Indiana. Second Church had pioneered a pastoral residency program under the leadership of their senior minister, William Enright, and a generous gift from church members Tom and Marjorie Lake. I immediately called Bill and asked if I could come to see him. He welcomed me warmly and shared what they had learned.[1] When we subsequently applied to the Lilly Endowment for a grant that would allow us to host a much larger program than we had foreseen with only our own resources, the model we emulated was the one Second Church had already employed. We have remodeled it somewhat over the years—the way anyone would remodel a house according to the living arrangements of the family that lives in it—but the basic architecture of the program has remained.

Over the years of operating residency programs, churches, regional groups, dioceses, and denominations have experimented with various models that continue to flourish. Some, like Wilshire, have moved from a program that is based solely in one church to a program that relates closely with other local churches. Wilshire has maintained the full breadth of its program in the process, but other congregations have scaled back on their own program and partnered with new congregations that have added residents. These will be described more fully below. Which model you choose to customize depends upon your unique circumstances, but descriptions of possible models and variations will help. While some of them are denominational and others ecumenical, all of them are based in the local church and are therefore worthy of your consideration as you begin construction of your own program.

The two basic blueprints of pastoral residency in a local congregation are the *solo resident* and the *multiple resident* models. Churches that start residency programs begin by calling one or more residents in a class for two to three years. Sometimes the resident class (whether one resident or more) will overlap with another class, sometimes not. How a church structures its program will depend partly on available resources, partly on church size, and partly on the scope of commitment the church is willing to make to the work. In either model, and in any variation on it, establishing a wider relationship to other churches doing residency work will greatly enhance the effort of the individual church.

Model A:
Solo Resident

A church might call one pastoral resident to serve on its staff for two years. Optimally, the resident will be a pastor without program assignments in any specific area that requires staff coverage. Pastors are generalists who attend to ministry across all ages and stages of life in the congregation. They are best prepared to do that work when they are trained in that way. We will look later at how to structure the work of a resident following this approach, but for now the concept is most important to establish. The pastoral resident should be added to the staff and function alongside the permanent pastor, in cooperation with any other staff. She will carry out all of the duties of a pastor, or as many of them as possible.

Two years has proven to be a time frame that well suits pastoral residency. It allows for considerable growth in the resident's practice of ministry as well as readiness to enter a congregation in a permanent position after the residency. Congregants consistently comment on the progress residents make from their first sermon to last, and often on improvements from sermon to sermon. The same is true of other pastoral functions, although preaching is the most visible to the most number of people. Program directors also observe a difference in confidence of young pastors that corresponds to their movement into the second year of residency.

Although one-year residencies would allow for training more pastors, they would lack the time necessary for significant maturation. And while three-year residencies would better establish pastors in their skills, the congregation may become too attached to and dependent upon that resident. The church has to remember that sending out the resident to a new church is as important in its calling as welcoming the resident and receiving his ministry. The two-year residency is therefore one foundation for an effective residency, but three dimensions of mentoring relationships are also critically important.

First, there is no adequate substitute for an engaged and experienced senior pastor who walks alongside the resident. Programs that have assigned an associate to be the primary mentor of residents have not been as effective. Since a key point of a pastoral residency is to prepare young ministers to be effective senior pastors themselves at some point, close interaction with a mentoring senior pastor is crucial for that formation.[2] A solo resident model especially requires this relationship with the senior pastor because the resident will not have peer residents on staff to interact with.

Peer resident collegiality is a second dimension of an effective residency program that requires imagination and initiative in the solo resident model. When a church has more than one resident, this peer learning naturally results; in a solo residency it must be created. One way to do so is by fostering peer relationships with ministers of the same generation, whether from the permanent staff of the residency church or from other churches locally. Residents frequently cite peer mentoring as a significant learning component of their experience. A more formal approach to providing this peer dimension is through a "cluster" relationship with one or more residency programs. Multiple residents in one church obviously covers the basic need for peer learning, but even in programs with multiple residents the evidence is building that wider interaction with

residents in other churches deepens the training. If you set out
to call one resident to your church, adding this dimension to
the structure of your program will maximize the mentoring
effect. Several approaches to this will be outlined below.

Third and finally, a strong lay mentoring team gives the
resident a view from the pew, so to speak. Since pastors partner
with laity in the daily work of building and sustaining healthy
churches, they need to practice that relationship during their
residency. We will take a closer look at creating strong lay
leadership teams in the next chapter.

Two Remodeling Options: Associate Minister or Resident Pastor

Money is sometimes a limiting factor when beginning a residency program, or it at least narrows the scope of what is
possible. The most cost-effective way of starting a pastoral
residency program is to convert a permanent staff position
into a residency. This will generally save the church money
in overall compensation, since a resident will be a less experienced pastor than someone the church otherwise might hire
for the position. A church can take an existing staff position
and fill it with a resident who will rotate out of that position
every few years, going on to a permanent role in that church
or another church thereafter.[3]

Ideally, an associate pastor position that includes duties
closest to that of a senior pastor should be chosen for this role.
The more the position simulates the duties of a senior pastor
the better prepared the resident will be to make the transition
to a senior pastor role. Hyde Park Union Church in Chicago
has a close relationship to Jackson Park Hospital, which is

located in a low-income neighborhood near the church. Hyde Park residents rotate during their two years between serving as chaplains to the hospital and doing outreach and children's work with the neighborhood. Chaplaincy work is closely related to the pastoral care ministry of a typical pastor, which makes the tie between these two arenas of ministry work for their program.

If the church has a broader view of training ministers that is not narrowly focused on the pastoral role, then assigning duties to the resident that permanent staff might otherwise handle is another route to take. For instance, a church might want to add a new ministry to young adults and call a resident to try to get that work started. Or, a church that hopes to strengthen a ministry to children or youth but cannot afford a commitment to a permanent staff position might call a resident to see if that work can lead to a full time staff need.[4] Most of the work that has been done in Transition into Ministry programs thus far has focused on training pastors, but what has been learned from these programs is transferrable to other ministerial roles.[5]

Before making any such a move toward converting a permanent staff position into a residency role, consider the hidden costs involved. While it may seem initially to be less expensive, residency requires greater oversight from and investment by existing staff and lay leaders. It may also require additional financial resources for professional coaching and training. A residency model demands more, not less, work from the senior pastor or supervising minister. The church should be prepared for a culture change within the staff and make allowances for the additional workload or shift in work emphasis.

Another variation to consider for smaller churches is the resident pastor model. Many smaller churches have functioned this way without knowing it for a long time. Most often they are located near a seminary or divinity school. They are solo pastor churches that have unofficially seen their job as training young pastors and sending them on. They have employed ministerial students on a part-time basis or allowed their full-time role to include seminary work. This usually has meant they were able to afford a pastor they otherwise could not afford, knowing that they would not be able to keep him long. If such churches were to become intentional about that work and formally adopt a residency model, they might extend their tradition profitably and enhance the effectiveness of their teaching role.

The same can be said for churches that have declined to the point of not being able to afford a full-time pastor. If the church could call a pastor who would understand her role as senior pastor in residence, or resident pastor, the church could turn a discouraging reality into a promising one. The church could literally reinvent itself as a teaching congregation that chooses its work of training pastors, rather than having it chosen for them by calling a part-time experienced minister to continue a diminished church program.

Hillcrest Baptist Church in Mobile, Alabama, has pioneered the resident pastor approach. After reaching a high of about 200 in worship attendance in their first decade of ministry, the church dwindled in number, resources, and enthusiasm due to pastoral conflicts, church splits, and part-time leadership from a semi-retired pastor over the next twenty years. In February of 2010, they called their first Resident Pastor. He functions as the solo staff member of the congregation that now numbers about 40 in weekly worship attendance. The church is attempting to take on the role of a teaching congregation. It created a relationship with our church in Dallas, whereby the pastor functions as a resident in an extended cohort with our Dallas residents. He travels to Dallas two or three times per year, and he joins the group regularly via video-conferencing for preaching and other pastoral seminars. The goal for the church is to inculcate this model in such a way that when this residency is completed, they will send off this well-trained young minister to another congregation and then begin the process again with a new resident pastor. In this case, the residency term is three years rather than two years, in order to establish more continuity for the church. The connection to another program like that of Wilshire's is a salient factor, but even if the church were only able to create a coaching relationship for the pastor and/or a peer learning group with other pastors, it would strengthen the effort beyond what the church could do by itself.[6]

Model B:
Multiple Residents

Churches with abundant resources may take the step of hosting more than one resident at a time. The system that works for a solo resident can be expanded to work for multiple residents. Additional lay leadership will be required, along with greater staff coordination and supervision. Scheduling for preaching, teaching, and pastoral care duties becomes more complicated. Yet the benefits of multiple residents are multiple.

If one resident adds to the life of the church, each additional resident adds to it exponentially.[7] Most residents are young clergy. Youth usually brings enthusiasm that more than balances inexperience. The church sees itself increasingly as being in the business of rearing skilled pastors more than just dabbling in it. And perhaps the greatest benefit is peer learning. Residents learn with each other and from each other in a collegial environment. They carry the value of collegial ministry with them when they leave, committed to nurturing friendships in ministry that last a lifetime. This byproduct of multiple resident programs may also become an antidote to clergy burnout in the long term, as a great deal of research suggests that loneliness in ministry contributes to a loss of vocational stamina.

Several patterns of multiple residents are possible. A church may call one new resident each year, thus maintaining a cohort of two residents with one coming in and one going out each year. The same pattern may hold with classes of two residents per year, resulting in a larger cohort of four. This approach keeps the learning wheel spinning for the congregation as well as the residents. Every year there will be a dependable rhythm of welcoming one or more new residents and sending out one or more. These rituals of receiving and sending reinforce the nature of the program as a short-term endeavor, and they help establish practices of hospitality and mission. The other advantages are for the residents themselves. Each year a class becomes senior and takes on an older-sibling sense of responsibility to the younger, entering class. This peer mentoring mirrors the mentoring of senior staff to all the residents, and it becomes another means for residents to practice for their own mentoring roles in their future churches. Moreover, because every cohort will relate in some way to three classes—the one ahead of theirs, their own, and the one behind—a broader connection to the program's alumni group will be more easily maintained over the years.

Another pattern for multiple residencies is a two-year cohort. Two or three residents enter the program together for two years, after which the church will call a fresh cohort to follow them. While there are fewer congregational rituals of welcome and sending in this model, there may be greater stability in the learning process. Residents will go through experiences together, rather than staggering the learning. This can also be easier on existing staff, since they will need to do their main mentoring work only once in a two-year span instead of annually. Some benefits of peer learning described in the staggered classes model will be missed in this approach, but the converse is also true: this model allows for deeper relationships to be formed over two years than the other model. Residents in a two-year cohort model will learn each other's personalities and work style better. This pattern of working together corresponds well to the permanent staff arrangements they will experience in future congregational ministry. And the church will be able to perceive the cohort as a group that is learning together, rather then having to distinguish between the more and less experienced residents.[8]

Multiple resident programs demand more of everyone involved than solo resident programs. Allocating preaching and teaching opportunities, committee assignments, and other duties will be more challenging. Larger churches with many ongoing programs will be a better fit for the multiple resident model than smaller family-size churches. Multiple resident programs will naturally be more expensive and require more administrative help. The beauty of them is seen in the many young pastors who will find their places all over the ecclesial map.

Clusters and Other Configurations

The solo resident and multiple resident models are the two standard configurations that have been tried and tested for congregations. Some churches, judicatories, and denominations have been building off of these residency models in creative ways. As mentioned earlier, these approaches have the great merit of adding a strong peer dimension to the residency experience.

This creative approach was pioneered in the Boston area. The Village Church in the Boston suburb of Wellesley (Wellesley Congregational Church) partnered with the Historic Charles Street Church in inner-city Boston. The Village Church is a predominantly white congregation in the United Church of Christ denomination, and Charles Street is a predominantly black church in the African Methodist Episcopal tradition. A residency cohort of four, with two residents from each church, was created, allowing the residents to get a taste of ministry in both urban and suburban settings. The churches have held services together periodically, and their pastors, supervising coordinators, and residents have worked closely to extend the residency experience.

In the Episcopal Diocese of Chicago, young ministers are placed in associate roles in ten congregations. These parishes and their experienced rectors were identified as being adept at mentoring. The resident associates, their mentors, and their congregations collaborate together in various ways to enhance the learning. An officer of the diocese coordinates the program.

The Christian Church (Disciples of Christ) has a residency-like mentoring program called the Bethany Fellowship.

Young ministers already serving in their first call are matched with experienced mentors. Twice-a-year retreats with peer pastors and monthly mentor conversations are the heart of the program.

In the Moorhead, Minnesota–Fargo, North Dakota area, greater Washington, D.C., New York City, and Boston, churches have created new "cluster" models within a denomination. Trinity Lutheran Church in Moorhead is the hub of a residency wheel that includes three residents at Trinity who serve two-year terms and two first-call pastors who serve smaller rural congregations without term limits. A similar denominational pattern is taking shape with Episcopal churches in New York City and the greater Washington, D.C., areas, emanating from the experienced work of St. James' Church in Manhattan and Christ Church in Alexandria, Virginia.

In Dallas, we have developed an ecumenical cluster that involves residents from several churches working together in an extended local cohort. Wilshire's cohort of four residents is joined now by a three-year resident pastor in Mobile and by two-year solo residents in two Presbyterian churches, a United Methodist church, and an Episcopal church.

One way to begin a residency program is to find an existing program near your church and pursue the question of a possible relationship to it. Programs have been operating in many cities and areas across the country in various denominations, ecumenically, or in conjunction with seminaries or divinity schools. For example, if a church in the Nashville area were interested in beginning a residency, it might try to coordinate its effort with the Disciples House at Vanderbilt Divinity School, which has conducted a comprehensive program for its students and graduates. The same is true in Atlanta where Central Presbyterian Church hosts a residency program and the Baptist-related McAfee School of Theology has sponsored solo residencies for their graduates in area churches.

Churches that are experimenting with this cluster model begin with a church or group that has already gained experience with its own program. The church calls its own resident, who then works both in the calling church and with peer residents in other cluster churches. While this likely works best in a geographically close configuration, ease of travel and communication today may make geography less important than intention and commitment.

On final thing in connecting residents with other residents: The Fund for Theological Education holds an annual national gathering of pastoral residents and sponsors other related events during the year that may enhance the residency experience. The Atlanta-based organization has a rich history extending back over half a century in nurturing the call to ministry in young people and in assisting churches in the training of them. They are also in the process of setting up a national residency network that will help resident alumni connect with one another and communicate.

How to Decide?

Imagine you have just walked through model homes in a planned community. You've seen some variations on the two basic models in the development. Before you decide to move in, you have to decide which model is right for your family of faith and how it might be customized to fit your unique situation.

More than likely you have already formed an exploratory committee or task force or some sort, whether formal or informal, to help you look into the possibility of beginning a pastoral residency program. If not, now is the time. The senior pastor and any staff members who would work closely with the residency program should be part of the group. Key laypersons—both elected and unelected—who have roles or expertise in any or all areas such as personnel, human resources, finance, and development should be added. Be sure to include longstanding church members in the group; their voices will carry weight.

When deciding how many residents the church may wish to host at a given time, consider the size of the church and the permanent staff, the staffing needs of the congregation, the capacity of existing staff to manage one or more resident colleagues, the aptitude for mentoring present in the church and staff, and possible connections to other local residency programs. In general churches with average Sunday attendance under 250 should focus on the solo resident model, while larger, multi-staff churches should consider the multiple-resident model. The goal is to right-size the program, to match the model with the church in a way that challenges the congregation and yet doesn't overwhelm it. The best model is the one that fits your church while also achieving the goal of forming well-prepared pastors.

Don't assume at the outset that your funding will be limited. Before finalizing a plan, pursue all potential funding sources. These will be explored in detail in a later chapter, but be sure to talk to foundations, denominations, seminaries, other churches with residency programs, as well as members with wealth and a generous spirit. Make sure you have adequate financial resources committed to whatever model is chosen for at least one iteration of a residency class.[9] "If you build it, they will come" is true for donors to a certain extent; that is, donors will often give better to something they see is working than to something only in the conceptual stage. But enthusiasm for the idea has to be matched to sufficient long-term funding, else the poet Robert Burns's lines be an unwelcome fate:

> The best laid schemes of mice and men
> Go often askew,
> And leave us nothing but grief and pain,
> For promised joy![10]

Chapter 3

Forming the Team

ENLISTING AND PREPARING THE MENTORING CAST

The African proverb says, "It takes a village to raise a child." Any parent knows what that means. Children don't enter the world fully formed. They aren't ready to take their place in the community and contribute to its well-being simply by the virtue of being born. And they certainly don't develop their innate gifts for leadership on their own. A whole ecology that consists of parents, grandparents, siblings, extended family, neighbors, friends, teachers, community leaders, and religious elders creates a culture that shapes the character and identity of each child. Each figure has a unique role to play in blessing, guiding, disciplining, nurturing, and calling forth the potential of the child. When the village colludes to that end, children are able to move through the necessary stages of development and take their place in leadership for the next generation.

Likewise, it takes a church to raise a pastor. The entire concept of a pastoral residency program is based on this collaborative conviction. Pastors are made, not born. They may be born with certain qualities that make them ripe for the work. But they will only know that about themselves, and they will only hone those gifts for effective service, within the context of a church that receives them, nurtures them, and sends them out to serve.

Jake Hall, a former Wilshire resident and current pastor of Heritage Baptist Fellowship in Canton, Georgia, uses the metaphor of a womb to describe this nurturing role of the church. "The space created by the residency program allowed my skills to develop and mature in real time, but from the safety of protected space. I was able to experience the full pulse of life in a congregation without the dangers of life outside the womb. There were mentors to model, a congregation to observe, and friendships that encouraged reflection. Life as a pastor would have been a premature birth at best without the pastoral residency experience."

Metaphors abound when talking about the culture of a congregation's residency program. I have sometimes called it a laboratory where young ministers can experiment before taking their gifts to market, so to speak. At other times I have talked about it being a launching pad for a young minister's upward call. Craig Dykstra of the Lilly Endowment has compared it to teaching a child to swim. He recalls lessons he learned during his seminary days as a swimming instructor for preschoolers at the local YMCA. The first step is to get the children to overcome their fear by getting them acclimated to the water. They have to learn to trust the buoyancy of the water that mysteriously holds them up and keeps them from sinking. The instructor first comes alongside them and leads them gently into the pool. He then puts his hands under them and gets them used to floating on their back, relaxing their muscles, and breathing. He finally removes his hands, and after some initial panic of realizing they are on their own, they are ready to learn to swim.[1]

We might extend the swim instructor metaphor a little further and say that pastoral residency work also moves the fledgling beyond simple trust in God's call and the church's blessing; it pushes them to perfect their gifts in the same way young swimmers have to learn to perfect their stroke, kicking motion, breathing technique, and all the while stay within their lane. It's a process that moves from one kind of support and encouragement to another, giving the novice pastors more freedom as they show themselves ready for it.

Regardless of what metaphor is chosen, the church that hosts an effective pastoral residency program will be a community that helps young ministers claim their identity as pastors, and at the same time grow in their confidence and competence in performing pastoral duties in order to flourish in the pastoral life.

Who then are the partners to be found and enlisted in this work within the local church and beyond, and what roles must they play? Five groups need to be formed and cultivated as a church develops its mentoring team for hosting a pastoral residency program: a church oversight committee, the staff leadership team, lay support persons, peer colleagues, and partners in the residency community.

A Church Oversight Committee

Whether decisions are made in your congregation by a session, an elder board, a deacon fellowship, a church council, a vestry, an administrative committee, or the whole church in conference, any new program needs advocacy from key influencers and approval through official channels. A good place to start in the creation of a pastoral residency program is in the formation of a group of interested and respected people to shepherd the process. The group may be formal or informal to begin with, but eventually it will help to have it authorized by the church to oversee the residency work.

The idea for hosting a residency program might come initially from the pastor or from key laypersons, but if it is to become the church's program it will need credibility with a broad constituency; otherwise, it will be a pet project of the pastor or of a few interested persons. It may be supported for a time but never rise above cameo status. As long as things go well, it will belong to the church, but when a resident acts inappropriately or fails to meet expectations, or when the church experiences financial challenges, it will be easy to dismiss the whole enterprise as a pet project of a few. An official oversight committee will authenticate the work and drive it toward the center of the church's life. It will strengthen the sense of ownership and stewardship the whole church feels for the residency program.

It may be tempting in the early stages of a residency program to bypass the creation of a new group to give oversight, relying instead on existing structures such as a church council or a pastor-parish relations committee. This could have the benefit of integrating the program with the full ministry of the church from the start, and legitimate oversight can certainly be achieved in that way, especially if the church has only one resident. But the larger the church's ambition for residency work, the greater the need for capacity building within the church. Residency work has an ecology of its own that will require a group that thinks only about its success.

Responsibilities for a pastoral residency oversight committee may include: setting policies for the program; developing a budget; providing supervision to the residents or counsel to the supervisors; helping with recruitment and evaluation; enlisting lay support persons; organizing welcoming and sending rituals; aiding fundraising efforts within the church and writing grant proposals for funding from other sources; keeping track of resident alumni and nurturing ongoing relationship between the alumni and church; and generally providing legitimacy for the program in the congregation. As you can see, there's enough to be done by such a committee to justify its existence as a separate group.

When organizing an oversight committee, use the congregation's normal process of enlistment. Many churches employ a nominating committee or a committee on committees to appoint those who will serve in official capacities. Nominators should look for a diverse group that will have a passion for the work. Like the exploratory committee discussed in the last chapter, this group—surely with many of the same people as that previous group—should include someone with a human relations background, another with fundraising skills; someone with administrative abilities, another with ministry experience; someone who has been mentored or has mentored others, another with educational training; someone with high respect in the church, and another with financial capacity to the sustain the program.

Linda Smith has served on the oversight committee of Wellesley Congregational Church for ten years. She points to the reciprocal blessing of her service. "Through meeting with the residents from the interview process through their two years in our midst, I have had the opportunity to watch each of them find their 'voice' and live into their calling to ministry in varied and wonderful ways. Having lay participants working actively with ministers new to a congregation, as well as to ministry, is a two-way blessing. The congregants have the opportunity to befriend and learn about what the minister is experiencing and offer support along the way. Having trusted 'go to' lay people is a comfort and support that all ministers need, but particularly ones new to the calling. My faith has grown and been nourished in countless ways through my involvement with our pastoral residents."

By nurturing the call of pastoral residents, a congregation nurtures God's call among all its members. The church becomes an incubator of ministers—clergy and lay, ordained and non-ordained.

Staff Leadership Team

Senior Pastor

Young ministers are eager to enter a pastoral residency program, largely because of the opportunity to work alongside an experienced senior pastor and staff. They hope that the unusual role of resident will give them distinctive insights into the daily routines of pastoral life. They want to pick the brain of the senior pastor. They want to understand what goes into sermon preparation, staff supervision, pastoral care, stewardship education, and congregational leadership.

The commitment of the senior pastor is crucial to the success of residency work, even if an associate is assigned to coordinate the daily oversight of the program. When the senior pastor plays a strong part in the process, residents benefit from the unique perspective of the one whose role they are training to one day play themselves. Only the pastor wakes up in the morning with the full weight of a congregation's mission on her mind. She alone has the vantage point of the whole from which to view the church's work. If she shares that vision effectively with the residents, they will begin to develop their own pastoral imagination.

Some programs assign an associate minister to take the lead with resident formation, while the senior pastor plays a supportive role due to the breadth of his other responsibilities and time constraints. Sometimes the lead mentor role is combined with the program coordinator position described below. Pastoral formation of residents will benefit from the lead mentor having pastoral credentials and experience, whether that be the senior pastor or an associate.

Either way, clergy mentoring of residents is crucial for the success of the program. The leadership of more than one clergy mentor can strengthen the experience because of their differences. Jana Reister, a former resident from the First Presbyterian Church in Ann Arbor, Michigan, makes that point: "The built-in mentoring of residents by the Rev. Budge Gere and the Rev. Melissa Anne Rogers was a key component to my thriving as a new pastor. Each is different in personality and ministry style, but both have a wealth of experience and were patient and supportive in their own ways."

Nancy Ferrell is a lay leader of the residency program at St. James' Episcopal Church in New York City. She knows firsthand the value of good lay leadership, but she insists that a key ingredient in the formation of excellent pastors is "the clergy mentor, who must have a willing attitude to teach, share knowledge and work, and offer guidance on any topic that may arise during the training period."

The clergy mentor has enormous power to bless and guide the residents in their development. Sometimes that involves a generous pat on the back, at other times a gentle kick on the backside. When a respected pastor acknowledges the growing gifts and graces in the resident, the young pastor can move beyond questions of pastoral identity and more freely operate as a pastor. On the other side, however, a young pastor needs to learn that he can't do whatever he likes and serve the church well. Just as there are rules to any game that must be followed in order to win, there are ways of being as a pastor that must be observed in order to build a strong ministry. Work organization, ways of handling conflict, and transparent relationships with colleagues and support staff are just a few of these habits of being that make or break a pastor. A clergy mentor has to be candid about these disciplines and insist on their development.

Program Coordinator

The senior pastor can be aided greatly in this work by a program coordinator, who may or may not be ordained clergy. Churches with multiple residents have found it helpful to have at least a part-time associate to coordinate the residency program. Many senior pastors are not as administratively skilled or don't have the time to devote to the work of daily scheduling, planning, evaluating, and reporting on the progress of the program. It may be possible to add this responsibility to the pastor's administrative assistant, especially if the church is hosting only one resident.

If the church participates in a local cluster program with other residencies, there may be a program coordinator in a larger program who can give administrative guidance. For example, Wilshire is the "mother church" to the Dallas cluster that includes four other local congregations, each with one resident. Our program coordinator, Geri McKenzie, has ably trained the administrators in the sister churches, and she coordinates the schedule of their joint interactions. In the Wellesley program, Chris Braudaway-Bauman has worked in tandem with Martin Copenhaver, the senior pastor. She has at the same time worked with the Massachusetts Conference of the United Church of Christ, helping to establish a peer-mentoring component for all newly ordained ministers.[2] From the start of their programs, St. James' in New York City and Christ Church in Alexandria, Virginia, assigned this role to associate rectors. They had the advantage of being experienced clergy mentors as well as coordinators of the program. Others who fill the program coordinator role have backgrounds in academic coaching or leadership development, human relations or corporate management.

Permanent Staff

Another important factor in a successful residency is to fit it seamlessly within the permanent staff. Central Presbyterian Church in Atlanta experienced some negative feedback after the first year of their residency program from existing staff that felt excluded from the mentoring process. Wilshire has likewise had to adjust the structure of the program to guard against the impression that the residents were something like a shadow staff. Residents should be part of the full ministerial staff from the beginning, learning to work alongside colleagues in ministry.

Permanent staff can add an important mentoring dimension. Residents who hope to become senior pastors will one day work with associates who serve in various program areas, such as children, youth, and adult education, music and worship, community ministries, and administration. Learning to see ministry from their point of view will help young pastors broaden their vision. Program associates often have tremendous experience and insight to offer young pastors.

Pastoral associates have gifts to offer the program that don't fit neatly into their own job description. Three examples from Wilshire illustrate this. Our associate pastor is a trained journalist and editor who coaches residents in pastoral writing, whether sermons, e-mails, or newsletter columns. Our music minister is well read in family systems theory, and he guides residents to see their families of origin, nuclear families, and church families in greater perspective. Our program coordinator is a trained coach in the Gallup StrengthsFinder Inventory of gifts. She counsels each resident about the ways their top five strengths may contribute well to their ministry and how they might view others they work with who have different strengths.[3]

Permanent staff may need training in order to understand mentoring. Residents are not merely extra hands to do more effective youth ministry. A former Wilshire children's minister saw residents mainly as available bus drivers, camp counselors, and Vacation Bible School workers. She did not know how to involve them as colleagues, walking alongside them and sharing her philosophy of ministry to children. Instead, a children's minister could discuss cognitive and faith development with residents, giving them a better sense of how to talk to children about what it means to believe or when and how a child might make a faith profession. The children's minister might include residents in a conference with a child or a child's parents as this subject is addressed. Staff has to learn how to mentor residents rather than simply using them to support their work.

SUPPORT STAFF

Finally, pastoral residents can learn a great deal from experienced support staff. Administrative assistants are vital players in the church's pastoral work. Young ministers are adept with cell phones, email, and other forms of communication. They are used to doing all their scheduling and personal contacts themselves. They have little or no experience working with support staff, whose job it is to help make pastors' ministries more effective. Residents can learn from support staff how to work in partnership with assistants in order to focus their own pastoral work on the things only they can do.

Lay Support Persons

LAY SUPPORT TEAM

In addition to an oversight committee that will include laypersons, most programs have created covenant groups or support teams made up entirely of laity. These are usually composed of five to seven people who meet periodically to pray for their assigned resident, give feedback and encouragement, help them get acclimated to the church and community, and learn about the pastoral life from the perspective of the pew.

Lay support team members covenant to attend events at church when their resident is serving; for example, when preaching, celebrating Communion, teaching a Bible study, or performing a baptism or wedding. Just being there for the resident is encouraging in itself, but it also gives the laypersons perspective that informs their feedback and puts substance to their presence.

A lay support team should represent the diversity of the church, balancing gender, age, marital status, and length of time as a member of the congregation. Consider including someone with the financial capacity to make a significant contribution to the work. A good experience with the residents may pave the way for later conversations about funding the program. It might help to have someone who has been an intern or resident in a law, business, or medical setting. Everyone enlisted should love the church and be a faithful and supportive member. Each should have something constructive to offer, but none should possess an overly critical spirit. A resident should come away from this experience with a positive view of the church, and especially of the relationship between pastor and people.

Once the program is up and running, church members become eager to be asked to serve on lay support teams. They hear stories from those who have served. They see the residency as one of the truly generative ministries of the church. Lay support team members become great advocates for the program throughout the church.

Most lay support teams meet six to ten times per year. Sometimes these meetings are unstructured, opening the agenda to whatever the resident or the team wants to discuss. The resident and the chair of the lay support team should work together on planning and sharing in the leadership of each meeting. These meetings will hone the residents' ability to work with committees in the future. Residents will learn the delicate dance of shared leadership in the church between clergy and laity. All involved will improve their listening and dialogue skills.

The lay support team is invaluable at giving a young minister an honest assessment of how church members view the church, the pastor, and key issues of ministry. Over time we have collected some profitable prompts for conversation that might be helpful as meeting agenda items. A few examples include:

- Visitation (whether hospital or home): Tell of your experiences with and your expectations of pastoral care visits.
- Stewardship: What are the best and worst ways of talking about giving?
- Conflict: What role should the pastor play in dealing with conflict in the church?
- Youthfulness: What are the perceptions of young clergy? How can a young pastor gain the trust of the congregation?
- Diversity: How comfortable are you with diversity of beliefs and standards of conduct within the church? How should a pastor best address these?
- Worship: What do you think are important ingredients in effective worship?
- Preaching: What makes a good sermon?
- Weddings and Funerals: What are the marks of good pastoral leadership in these critical moments of joy and sorrow?
- Governance: What does it feel like to work with the pastor or staff on a committee or in a decision-making group? What are the proper roles of clergy and laity?

- Pet Peeves: Name some things about church life in general and pastors in particular that you hold in high or low esteem.

A lay support team can also be a useful group to act as a mock search committee, preparing the young minister for the candidating process ahead.

Additional Lay Contributors

Some churches enlist host families and faith partners in addition to the lay support team. Host families focus on hospitality. They make sure residents feel at home in their new church and community. They invite them over for holidays, take them to lunch, offer tickets to local events, and help them find things like a veterinarian or an auto mechanic. They often host the residents in their home when they later return to the church as alumni for reunions or other events.

Faith partners focus on spiritual friendship. Sometimes their role is only to meet periodically to listen to the resident and pray together. Sometimes they encourage one another's spiritual practices, holding each other accountable for nurturing their spiritual lives. At Wilshire, we've found that this works best when residents choose their own faith partner, in consultation with their supervisors. This usually occurs after about three to four months in the program, when residents have been able to identify someone with whom they have rapport, for whom they have respect, and in whom they have confidence.

In addition to the lay support team, host families, and faith partners, a number of professionals might be enlisted to serve consultatively in their fields. An accountant may give tax and other personal financial advice. A medical doctor, a dentist, and a therapist might agree to see the residents on a reduced fee basis or for free. A marriage and family therapist can be particularly helpful to residents as they navigate the early transitions they are experiencing in their personal and professional lives. A family therapist does just that for Wilshire residents. She has the advantage of being the wife of a man who served several churches in an associate pastor role. Her gift to the residents is to offer three free sessions for them as individuals or as couples.

TESTIMONIES TO LAY INVOLVEMENT

Beautiful stories come out of the contributions of laypersons to residents and vice versa. Lay support team members keep up with the young ministers beyond their time at the residency church. They feel a stake in their ministry and sometimes even travel to their new church to encourage them. Residents often do the same with them.

Linda Hoepner served on a lay support team for a female resident at St. Paul's Lutheran Church in Davenport, Iowa. "A wonderful friendship (for both me and my husband) grew from this. We attended her out-of-state wedding, became friends with her parents and husband. Our young resident has been gone for over two years yet we still stay in regular contact with her and her husband and feel a lifelong friendship has been formed. We often feel she has mentored and befriended us as much as we have to her."

Stories like Linda's are commonplace. Residents have their own tales to tell about laypersons who have gone above and beyond expectations to buy professional clothing for them, subsidize the cost of doctoral work, or take an interest in their children. One host family at Wilshire made sure to design a room in the new house they were building with their former resident in mind, knowing he would be coming back for annual reunions and other visits. They actually call it his room. The children of a man who had served on a lay support team gave a donation in his name after his death. The money is to be used for all new residents to buy a pair of well-made shoes for professional use. He had been a shoe salesman, and his kids saw this as a way of honoring his legacy.

Amy Grizzle, a former Wilshire resident, is now serving as an associate minister at the South Main Baptist Church in Houston. She tells the resident side of the story: "Having a lay mentoring team was an important part of my residency experience. It was a blessing to have a lay group surrounding me with love, encouragement and constructive feedback. A minister's job is to serve the church, and we are paid employees, so some might not value needing to affirm or encourage an employee in doing her job as that's not always a model highly valued in the corporate world. Yet, even as an employee and church leader, the church is my church family as well; to have someone tell me that they are holding me in prayer or walking with me in a difficult time means the world and enables me to experience church even as I serve it and help nurture that church family for others. To this day, I hear from my lay mentoring team with notes or emails or Facebook messages of encouragement. I continue to be thankful for their nurture of and investment in my ministerial formation."

The relationships made between young ministers and laypersons during the residency time do much to build spiritual bonds between clergy and laity. They help to dispel suspicions on both sides that would otherwise undermine the health of the church, and instead they greatly contribute to the church's well being across time.

Peer Colleagues

It may seem strange to include peer colleagues in the mentoring team. We tend to think that only older and more experienced ministers can be mentors. But the testimony of residents is clear that they learn a great deal from one another.

Marriage and family therapists point to relationships with siblings growing up as being more formative in preparation for marriage than watching the relationship their parents have with each other. The theory suggests that since marriage generally involves living with a peer in age and life experience, sibling relationships and friendships are the closest parallel. Likewise in ministry, we can learn a great deal from peers who are going through the same things as we.

Churches that host more than one resident at a time have a built-in advantage in the peer-mentoring component. Residents walk through the same duties and challenges together. They can learn to depend upon each other, push each other to be their best, and assure and console each other as need be. If the residency structure involves staggered classes, the senior resident colleague(s) can offer older sibling help to the first-year class.

If a church has only one resident, program leaders and the resident should make deliberate attempts to create peer relationships for the resident. One way to do so is by contacting other churches that host residency programs and looking for ways to communicate and possibly collaborate. Residents across the country attend gatherings and conferences together from time to time. Learning about and attending these events will give solo residents (and multiple residents) new peer learning opportunities.

If peer learning relationships with other residents becomes impossible or impractical, an alternative would be to establish relationships with young clergy in the community. Young ministers, especially those in their first call, may have much in common with residents. Residents can learn from first-call peers about transition into their first full-time church, about hidden pitfalls to watch out for, and a host of other things. Many first-call ministers, for their part, have said that they wished they had the opportunity to be residents, and so they can learn from those who are.

One former resident summed up her experience with peers this way: "One of the most formative and cherished facets of my residency experience was the opportunity to form collegial and collaborative relationships with my residency peers. For one year of my two, I was the only female with four other male residents; I felt valued as an equal and grew to consider my resident peers not only my valued colleagues, but also my brothers. Beyond the friendships formed, we continue to be a network of collegial support, formation, and resource for one another. We continue to stay in touch about life in general (we continue the healthy competition of a fantasy football league); we also network with each other about job placement possibilities both for ourselves and other openings at our various places of service. We maintain a Facebook group that is a place of sharing funny stories, sad experiences, great church leadership ideas, or words of wisdom and inspiration we have found valuable."

Partners in the Residency Community

Mentoring involves learning by residents and program leaders alike. For the residents, relationships with residents in other church programs can give them a broader perspective and help to expand their formation. They can compare experiences. They can share experiences. In doing so, they can identify areas of strengths and weaknesses in their own residency. They may be able to seek additional help beyond the limitations of the church they are serving.

Similarly, leaders of residency programs can learn from one another. Program leaders do their best within their own context, but they don't always know what possibilities exist beyond that context. They can get ideas and share some of their own. They can learn about evaluation methods, recruitment, lay enlistment, and every other subject covered in this book. But mostly, they will gain partners in the work and the confidence that they are a part of something larger than themselves, a movement that God may be engineering in and through them.

The Fund for Theological Education (FTE) is a good first contact to learn about other residency programs and gatherings throughout the year that might be profitable to attend. FTE not only coordinates the Transition into Ministry program for the Lilly Endowment, it also keeps up with alumni of those programs and tracks the work of others who are attempting residencies outside the Lilly community. Two other places to look are denominational judicatories and seminaries. As mentioned in the last chapter, denominational bodies—both national and regional—have experimented with different residency models, as have some seminaries. It may be possible to become part of their programs in some way.

~

In sum, a fertile mentoring culture includes a congregational oversight committee to ground the program in the life of the church. It is nurtured by accessible and attentive pastoral leadership and a program coordinator who keeps residents on track in addressing all the ministry practices that will prepare them well for their next call. Permanent staff—both clergy and lay, both program ministers and support personnel— extends the collegial spirit of the pastoral life for the resident. Laypersons provide an important mirror in which the young ministers can view their role. They allow the residents to begin to develop the necessary rapport with a congregation that is essential to a strong and significant ministry. Peer mentor relationships, whether within a multiple resident church or in the local or wider community, add a dimension of learning that builds collegiality and lays a foundation of friendship for the long haul of ministry. And finally, connecting the program itself to the larger movement keeps every aspect of the work honed.

Just as in a village or a family, there are complex generational and positional relationships to account for in any congregation. The experience of working with staff leaders, ministry colleagues, peers in residency, and laypersons with official and nonofficial roles allows residents to locate themselves within the congregational system and learn how to be nimble in navigating these diverse relationships.

Chapter 4

Recruiting Residents

DISCOVERING AND CALLING PASTORS WITH PROMISE

"Best and brightest, come away!"

Percy Bysshe Shelley's compelling line from his poem "The Invitation" describes also the yearning of churches for their future clergy. When we set out to recruit residents for pastoral ministry programs, we want the best and brightest. We don't want second-tier intellect or imagination, character or class. We want the next generation of ministers to honor the profession and lead the church well.

Intelligence is not a naked concept, though. As researchers have shown, there are various types of intelligence, and emotional intelligence is at least as important as the capacity to make good grades in school on exams that test knowledge of facts.[1] For example, a ministerial student with a middling academic record may have a brilliant capacity to maintain composure in a stressful situation that aids a church through times of conflict. This is a valuable quality for a pastor, at least as important as whether she has a firm grasp on the circumstances that led to the English Reformation under Henry VIII.

Congregations want smart pastors. They should expect that their pastor knows his field and can guide them well in matters of biblical interpretation and church history, to name just two areas. But "the best and the brightest" mentality can lead a church astray if it isn't carefully examined. It can lead to residents who become ministers of churches without the sufficient ministerial graces or pastoral passion to lead them well.

When David Halberstam sought to explain the origins of the Vietnam War, he borrowed that line from Shelley's poem for the title of his book, *The Best and the Brightest.* Halberstam applied the phrase to the so-called "whiz kids" that President John F. Kennedy brought into his administration—Ivy League educated mostly, leaders of industry and the academy whose supposedly brilliant policies often defied common sense and the wisdom of career State Department officials. They somehow knew better than those who had labored long in anonymity to understand geopolitical dynamics, and their arrogance produced the long and painful period of engagement in Indochina that stole many American lives and robbed the country of confidence in its leaders.[2]

Pastoral residency work, though, is not remedial learning for those who didn't absorb it in school and thus need a little extra training before they're foisted upon unsuspecting parishioners. Few churches have the will or the resources to initiate residency programs; the few that do want to find residents with potential for transformational good.[3] They want to discover candidates who can lead congregations in ways that honor the life of the church they inherit, add to it on their watch, and pass it on to another generation when the time comes.

So, what are those best and brightest attributes we should search for in resident candidates? And how do we locate these promising pastors?

Aptitude and Appetite

Aptitude and appetite are twin measurements to consider in choosing residents. Aptitude looks at gifts that allow one to perform ministry capably. Appetite looks at passion for ministry that allows one to perform ably. Aptitude looks at skills, appetite at art. Aptitude concerns the work of one's hands, so to speak, while appetite looks at whether one has the heart for it all. Aptitude makes it possible for you to do something; appetite makes you want to do it. Aptitude gets to the question of occupation, appetite to preoccupation—which essentially defines the difference between a job and a vocation.

A pastor with aptitude for the ministry but without an appetite for it may cast a chill over the heart of a congregation. A pastor with plenty of passion for the work, but who lacks the skills to perform the role with grace, may leave a congregation flailing in the shallows instead of moving deeper into the faith. Both aptitude and appetite are important.

To cite a biblical example, Saul had the aptitude to lead Israel, as did his successor David; but David also had the appetite for it. When the prophet Samuel tells Saul that God has called "a man after [God's] own heart" to succeed him as king, we aren't told what that means (1 Sam. 13:14). The narrator still leaves us guessing three chapters later about what counted in David for him to be called as the future king. All we are told is that mortals "look on the outward appearance, but the

Lord looks on the heart" (1 Sam. 16:7). Apparently, having heart matters to God. And having a heart for the work of serving the people is surely part of it.

Saul and David each had qualities of leadership that allowed them to fulfill their role, yet David is celebrated as a model figure to be emulated. So how do we discern the difference between them? Both Saul and David were kings of Israel, but the story subtly suggests that Saul was *King* of Israel, while David was King of *Israel*. David embodied the hopes and dreams of the people and saw his welfare and theirs as one thing, not two.

David wasn't perfect. No leader is. Pastors aren't perfect, but they are more likely to be successful if they sense the joys and sorrows of their life and their church's life as being bound together in some kind of spiritual union. So before addressing particular gifts and passions that make one more or less likely to succeed in congregational work, one defining mark of good resident candidates must be their sense of calling to serve the people of God.

Calling to Church Work

The church talks about ministry as a calling, but ministry can happen in many venues other than the pastoral office in a congregation. Residency is a wonderful stage on which a young minister may clarify the calling to pastoral work in a congregation. But a church needs to ask itself in the candidate search process how comfortable it will be with residents who go through the program only to discern that the pastoral life is not for them.

No one has perfect clarity about the mind of God or the claim of Christ at any given moment, because faith always deals as much with what we don't know as with what we do know. It's only in the wading in that we learn to swim. So, candidates who are not completely certain about their call to the pastorate but who have reason to probe further should be considered strongly. A successful residency will lead a young minister who believes he is called to be a pastor to discover the joy of being called Pastor. And that can only happen in the context of pastoral practice.

Returning once again to the medical model, students go through rotations during the latter part of their training that allows them to intern in different medical disciplines. When they graduate from medical school and apply for residencies, they do so for the specific area of medicine they intend to practice. Similarly, young ministers applying for residency should intend to serve as pastors.

It may seem odd to church members that all seminarians are not heading toward congregational ministry, but there are numerous fields of ministry to consider. Many young people today enter theological schools after discerning a call to ministry through involvement with parachurch groups. They have had little formation in local churches and sometimes carry no denominational identity. So the assumption that they will serve a congregation is not always present. Fortunately, internships conducted by local churches often help seminarians discern a calling to serve in congregational life. Many seminarians report that they clarified their call to serve a congregation during one of these field education opportunities.[4]

Churches that host pastoral residency programs prefer that the investment they make in young ministers translate into a lifetime of service to congregations like their own. Other churches may do the work of training leaders for community benevolences, justice organizations, campus ministries, chaplaincies, or teaching careers, but churches that sponsor pastoral residency programs hope to see our residents serving congregations for years to come.

Whether through written responses to questions, or by answers given in personal interviews, candidates should be able to articulate a sense of call to pastoral ministry. They should be able to say how they view the church's role in God's work in the world and why they believe they are best called to help the church accomplish that role. When candidates apply for the residency program, a statement of call should be included along with whatever record of educational and work history is outlined.

A prompting question—whether for a written essay or a personal interview—could range from the somewhat leading to the very specific. For example, "Tell us about how an experience you have had with a congregation has shaped your call to ministry?" Or, "How have you come to discern that your calling to ministry involves a calling to serve a congregation as a pastor?" You might ask, "Who have been your most significant models for ministry?" If the candidate does not cite a pastor or youth minister, say, it might require some follow-up to uncover whether there is real imagination for church work. Gary Simpson, Pastor of Concord Baptist Church of Christ in Brooklyn, asks candidates, "Who is your pastor?" If they cannot tell about anyone in particular who has been a role model or mentor, it makes it difficult to imagine that they have a deeply rooted experience in the church, which may be a liability in claiming a pastoral identity.

Qualities to Look For

Markers of Promise

Qualities that make a good pastor also make a good resident.

Melissa Wiginton, of the Fund for Theological Education, has identified five "markers" that portend ministry effectiveness,[5] to which I will add two more. The church is a people who belong to the community of Christ and live under the reign of God. So it must have leaders who reflect the values of the gospel. Wiginton lists these as: an inner life, a sense of wonder, an appreciation of ritual, connectionality, and engagement for healing the world.

An Inner Life

The pastorate is spiritual work and therefore requires a developing feel for the Spirit. A life of prayer, the capacity for solitude, habits of reflection like journaling or writing poetry, and spiritual reading all constitute evidence of a vital inner life. Pastors who will speak for God—no matter our qualifications of that claim—must have a sense that God is first speaking to them. Asking a candidate about her spiritual practices will open up a window into the soul.

A Sense of Wonder

The poet Rod Jellema talks about a kind of "double vision" with which one can look at one thing and see another.[6] Pastors and poets both need this quality. This spiritual seeing may be cultivated by an engagement with the arts, or by experiences of travel (literally or figuratively) that open the eyes to social locations and human experience different from one's own. So much of our culture is geared toward the mastery of data. Ministry involves rich participation in the mysteries of the world that God has made, mysteries that may be embraced but never controlled or manipulated for political or economic purposes. A question that probes the candidate to reflect upon a time when he was confronted with a cultural or ethnic difference that challenged him spiritually might help to reveal his capacity to embrace the mystery of "otherness" so crucial to the missional character of church leadership.

An Appreciation of Ritual

Ministers employ symbols and ceremonies to point beyond what we can all "see, touch, eat, or purchase," as Wiginton puts it. Reality is never exhausted in the things themselves. Rather, certain things have the power to point beyond themselves to meanings that can shape us and conform us to God's presence and work in the world. The symbol of the cross reminds us not only of the instrument of Christ death, but also of our own call to carry the suffering of the world and to bear it redemptively. Water baptism threatens our sense of immortality by reminding us that all our striving is losing in the end, but it also promises us that intentionally losing our life for the sake of the gospel brings new birth. The bread and wine of Communion nourish the spirit as well as the body. These morsels of meal become to us who receive them in faith a banquet of the body and blood of Christ. They feed us till we want no more, to paraphrase the old hymn.[7] But all of these are only ideas until they are enacted. If the people are to experience these with spiritual senses, we who administer these rituals must ourselves believe that we hold the holy in our hands, and do so with awe and humility. A question might be formulated to a candidate to discern her liturgical sensibilities and see if they match the church's practice.

Connectionality

An admittedly cumbersome word, connectionality doesn't suggest a social networking savant who knows how to turn Facebook into a ministry tool. Connectionality describes someone who understands that spiritual truth is relational and isn't pursued well alone. Pastors need to know that we don't know everything ourselves simply by being theologically educated and anointed as spiritual leaders of the community. We understand that there is great wisdom in the community itself. We know how to be in touch with the people, to listen to them, and to put them in touch with each other as a way of nurturing a spirit of discovery in the church. Young ministers are often taught in seminary that they need to maintain clear boundaries of privacy in order to have a healthy career, but sometimes this can lead to walls that prevent the people from getting close to the minister. A question that addresses how the candidate manages alone time and people time, work and play, may get at this issue of a candidate's relational capacity for pastoral ministry.

Engagement for Healing the World

Ministry in the name of Christ identifies with victims, standing with and for the weak and vulnerable. Aspiring pastors do not pursue a life of privilege up until the moment of their calling and then suddenly become champions of those on the underside of society. Potential residents should have some history of missional service that has formed their self-understanding. This may have come from their own family of origin in which suffering and misfortune were learned to be challenges that touched them personally. Or they may have internalized this by volunteer work or mission trips that introduced them to the world of the poor and dispossessed in neighborhoods far from their own. Churches looking for pastoral residents will want to see some evidence of incarnational ministry in the candidates' commitment to the healing of the world.

These five markers are not an exhaustive list in searching for candidates with the aptitude and appetite for the pastoral life. Two others have arisen from the accumulated wisdom of those who have pioneered pastoral residency work.

A Teachable Spirit

Residents enter into a mentoring relationship with a seasoned pastor, often with a dedicated staff, and always with a congregation that knows more about the ministry than it knows it knows. A teachable spirit in the resident is indispensable to a successful residency. Residents will only learn what they are open to learning. Where a teachable spirit is present, great things are possible. The questions asked during the recruiting phase can help shape the residents' expectations. In this regard, a question such as, "What do you hope to learn during your residency?" or "What areas of pastoral work do you think need special attention in your training?" To get a sense of whether the candidate is thinking beyond himself, you might ask, "How would you like the church to be different because of your residency?" or "What would you hope to leave behind at this church when you leave the residency?" These might help both the candidate and the church anticipate the contributions each could make toward the other.

Resiliency. Residents will receive criticism—positive and negative—from many sources: pastoral mentors, peer colleagues, and the members of the congregation at large. Candidates should be self-conscious about their ability to receive feedback appreciatively. They should also have the gumption to push back and engage mentors in some give-and-take that will foster greater mutual learning. Thus they need the proper combination of a strong sense of self and humility. Asking a candidate to describe a time when criticism helped him or when a failure aided her in growth might give insight into the readiness of the resident to receive feedback.

ADDITIONAL FACTORS

While these seven markers apply to the candidates for residency, the process of calling should also cause some reflection by the search committee. A candidate, for instance, may be excellent for a church other than the one to which she has applied. A search committee, however, has to be honest with itself about that fit. Furthermore, all the due diligence may add up to one conclusion, but a final decision will have to include a committee's innate sense of "rightness" before issuing a call. Thus, two other factors should be considered:

• *Compatibility.* Churches should look for a good fit with residents they call. Theological compatibility makes growth in reflective practice more likely. While some theological diversity is valuable, too much will compete with the goal of pastoral formation. The same is true with ecclesial compatibility. These days, models of church are legion, with some traditional and sacramental, others evangelical and nonsacramental, and still others emergent and either sacramental or nonsacramental. Finding residents who will eagerly learn the ways of ministry your church features will maximize the experience.

• *Intuition.* Finally, there's an intangible intuition that should be honored. Pastors and search committees, who are assigned the task of discerning whom to call as a resident, should attend to the feelings they have in the interview process. In his provocative book on decision making, *Blink: The Power of Thinking Without Thinking,* Malcolm Gladwell gives credit to the ability of people to size up situations and make good judgments in just minutes by use of what he calls the "adaptive unconscious" rather than through complicated analytics.[8] Although mistakes can be also be made in trusting educated instinct, his point is that more credit should be given to this mode of discernment than often is. In addition to all the data reviewed, a committee should look for that "it" factor that is hard to define but also hard to deny. That "it" factor may best be judged by the old adage, "I'll know it when I see." Different ways of putting the question might be: "Is this a person I want to spend the next two years with?" or, "Do I think our church would relish the chance to know and nurture this person in residency?"

That seems like a lot to consider, I know. No process will be perfect, just as no resident, no pastor, and no church is perfect. We are looking for real human beings who have some gifts that are suitable for the work, but mostly who have a driving desire for the church to be its best. It's impossible to manufacture all the perfect gifts for ministry and form them into an ideal resident. But the good news is that whomever God calls God also equips with both the gifts and graces to serve the church effectively. The church's job is to discover who has that call and those gifts and to hone them for better congregational service.

Where and How to Find Candidates

Willie Sutton said he robbed banks because that's where the money was. It's not quite as easy to figure where to pluck up good residents. Most churches go first to the seminaries and divinity schools associated in some way with their denomination. That's where the fledgling ministers are, we reason. And that is a good first stop in the search process.

Churches may call on seminary presidents or divinity school deans to find out who might be ripe among the graduating class for this work. Sometimes a professor or placement officer will offer suggestions. But these only know students in narrow contexts that don't always reflect what we are looking for in potential residents.

For example, one resident who joined our cohort from a renowned divinity school had excellent grades and knew how to say the right things about his desire for mentoring. He got excellent reviews from faculty and staff. But they had never witnessed him in social settings outside the academy. They could not have known that he would show up at his first staff meeting with an old ball cap on his head or miss an appointment with his supervisor because he was working out that morning and lost track of the time. No one bats 1.000 in the game of personnel recruitment, but experiences like this help us learn what to look for and what to ask about.

Sometimes the best residents have already been serving a church in an associate role for a few years. They may have been youth or college ministers and now sense they need better formation to make the jump to the pastorate. Judicatory leaders or fellow pastors may help locate these promising candidates.

Some churches employ their oversight committee of laity and clergy to conduct the search and call process. Others operate informally, including the supervising pastor, the program director (if there is one), and sometimes the current residents. Including current residents in the process adds one more learning experience to the residency, as future pastors will need to know how to select new staff colleagues.

Once a pool of candidates is identified and an initial screening is done, a process of deepening discernment begins. Most churches ask candidates to send written answers to questions that help determine articulation, clarity, passion, self-awareness, theological and ecclesial fit, and writing ability. While some questions have already been suggested in this chapter, others might address a person's faith journey, a life experience that helped shape Christian sympathy for people in need, reflections on lessons from family of origin, examples of collaborative work, or how criticism from some source has aided in personal growth.

A conference conversation with the selection committee usually follows the written stage of the process. This often helps to clarify written answers and probe other areas. Finally, a personal visit takes place. The church and the candidates can gain only so much over the phone or through written communication. Meeting in person allows the church to sense whether candidates would fit well, and it allows the candidates to see whether it feels right to them. It also gives the church and candidates a chance to evaluate how candidates might relate to other residents and/or permanent staff.

Before an offer is extended, the church should ask permission of the candidates to do routine criminal background and financial checks. These must be kept confidential, but they might turn up unexpected information that should be dealt with before the employment relationship begins.

∼

When all is said and done, welcoming new residents into the church renews the spirit of the congregation every time it happens. The church gains hope for the future and finds new energy for the work God has given it to do.

Chapter 5

Simulating Ministry

PATTERNING THE PASTORAL LIFE

My late father-in-law was an airline pilot for the now-defunct National Airlines. He flew DC-10s cross-country in his last years in the cockpit. New pilots were certified to fly National's planes at a training center in Miami. Every pilot who wanted to step up to newer or larger planes had to go through flight training there. Even the most experienced pilots, though, had to go through continuous training to maintain their license to fly because the lives of so many were at stake every time they took off.

The airline industry utilizes sophisticated simulation machines to train their pilots. On one occasion my father-in-law smuggled me into the training center after hours. He showed me the DC-10 simulator and put me in the pilot seat. The cockpit was an exact replica of the actual plane, but the windshield was a computer screen that displayed images of airports and runways, along with routes to destinations that included various weather conditions. Sitting there, I was able to simulate takeoffs and landings, controlling the plane as if it were real. But being an inexperienced flyer, I repeatedly crashed the plane in the simulation. The cockpit shook each time I crashed in order to let me experience my incompetence in a nonlethal way. But the good thing was that the computer could be immediately reset and we could try again, having learned from the failure without undue damage or loss of life.

A pastoral residency program seeks to simulate the pastoral life in a similar way. We design the resident's experiences in ways that track the actual rhythm of parish pastoral life, with all its regular and irregular patterns. Residents are trained in clear weather conditions, so to speak, and also in inclement weather. They learn to do the work of the pastorate that follows a predictable schedule, and then they learn to adjust to the unpredictable interruptions that constitute the real-time life of a pastor. They get to do all of this without the added pressure of carrying the full weight of the life of the church in their hands. Of course, pastoral residency is not carried out in a simulation machine; it's done with real people in actual ministry settings, but the church has agreed ahead of time to function in this way as a training center.

The Rhythm and Flow of the Residency

When you design the pastoral residency program of your church, the more closely you can simulate the actual life of a pastor the better. A "transition into ministry" program seeks to create the rhythm of a pastor's work, which allows the resident to live into the life of *ministry*. Equally important, however, is the flow of the program, which addresses the notion of *transition*.

Rhythm

Establishing a rhythm for the work week, for allocating time to duties, and for balancing work and personal life is one aspect of this training. Pastors tend to do their work in regular weekly patterns. For example, they may use their mornings for study and their afternoons for office work, appointments, and hospital visitation. They may set aside Tuesday mornings for staff meeting and all day Thursday for sermon preparation. They need to discipline themselves to observe a sabbath and keep it holy, something pastors are notoriously poor at doing because Sunday is a work day for us. The predictable rhythm of the work week is something residents have to learn in order to settle into the pastoral role and not be tossed to and fro by the winds of whim. Interruptions in the schedule—emergency medical crises or other urgent pastoral care needs—may be occasions of the Spirit, but they are only interruptions once a schedule has been established.

The transition into full-time employment from seminary life is sometimes challenging for young ministers, as they have to adopt new work patterns. Residents who have been in the work world before coming to church work may make this transition easier than those fresh from an academic environment. The vocation of pastor requires a high level of self-management. Pastors have to plan ahead, discipline their time, and pace their workload with respect to other responsibilities to family and self. Many residents may already have developed good self-management skills, but the church environment is a new dimension that requires them to be responsible to a community of staff and laypeople.

Senior pastors often work at home during part of the week, since much of their time is spent reading, studying, and writing, all of which is difficult to do in the church office. Residents will also need preparation time for sermons and other assignments. Some flexibility in office hours should be considered in the normal rhythm of the work week. Meetings and appointments will require residents to be present, on time, and prepared. These expectations should be made clear at the outset of the program. Other matters, such as expected professional dress, ways of responding in a timely fashion to phone calls and emails, what are proper modes of communication for what circumstances (for instance, when texting is appropriate and when it is not), also should be covered early in the program.

FLOW

Residents have chosen not to go straight into a first call. They have made this stop in the vocational journey in order to prepare themselves more completely for pastoral work. Therefore, a church's transition into ministry program will grant residents increasing responsibility as they grow in their capacity to handle it.

The span of the residency allows adequate time for this maturation process, but it has to be deliberately constructed to that end. If the resident is only used for additional staff labor as a summer intern might be, she will not be ready to be a pastor when she leaves the program. Likewise, if the resident is put in situations of responsibility beyond his training too quickly, the prospect of failure might damage his confidence and the confidence of the church in his ability. The church will want to find the right balance of responsible practice for young pastors that will help them be ready to fly solo in a pastorate of their own at the end of the residency term.

The overall flow of a two-year program should point toward increasing responsibility. The program will begin with a period of orientation that helps the resident become quickly acquainted with the culture of the church, the schedule of the services and meetings, relationships with staff and other residents, initial meetings with lay support persons, and planning for first ventures in preaching, teaching, and pastoral care. All of this will have to take place while getting settled in a new community, and all that that entails: making a house a home, getting new tags for cars, registering to vote, learning their way around, and a host of other things.

The first year features lots of firsts. It's not uncommon for a promising resident to confess doubt to his supervisor during the initial months. Moving from seminary to church, from student to minister, is somewhat disorienting. Residents have to push through these moments of insecurity until they find their vocational confidence. They have to learn the ropes before they can master them. Supervisors do well to design their work in accord with this trajectory.

Something remarkable happens toward the end of the first year: residents begin to take on the bearing of pastors. They begin to sense that this is who they are, not just what they do. The second year of residency reminds me of the Roman god Janus. Janus is the god of doorways or gateways—the god of transitions. He is pictured looking both ways, backward and forward. Likewise, second-year residents come into their own at the residency church. They are trusted with more responsibility. At the same time, however, they sense the clock ticking. They know they need to prepare for leaving. They start in

earnest to make themselves known to churches and judicatories in hopes of securing a call at the end of their residency. The residency church needs to allow for that bifurcated
reality by being firm about the need to work well where they
are and gentle in remembering that the point is also to send
them out.

The Principle of Reflective Practice

Churches that conduct pastoral residency programs, along
with judicatories that have their own version of first-call
mentoring for young clergy, have this in common: they move
the resident steadily toward the captain seat of pastoral leadership by utilizing various forms of learning that incorporate
different intensities of practice and reflection:

- Observe and reflect
- Participate and reflect
- Lead and reflect

These three modes of pastoral practice take residents deeper
into the pastoral life as they move the young ministers toward
fuller and firmer pastoral formation. By the time they leave
the program, residents should be prepared to lead a congregation from the seat of pastoral authority with competence and
confidence.

The *observe-and-reflect* mode of learning should be the least
utilized in a residency program. It may be the most common
approach to internships, and churches that have operated
internship and field education programs before adopting a
residency model will need to modify their approach in order

to achieve the goal of fully training a pastor. Most residents will already have experienced church ministry by observation. They will have watched pastors and other associates do their work, and they will likely have reflected upon that work with those more experienced ministers.

Observation is better than nothing. If a resident can only observe a pastor doing crisis care, that will be better than missing the experience altogether. But mentors should look for every opportunity to include resident participation in ministry moments of every kind. For instance, when a pastor visits with a couple in a premarital setting to discuss their upcoming wedding or with a family that is planning the funeral or memorial service for a loved one, the pastor might suggest to the resident ahead of time ways to contribute to the conversation rather than simply being present in the room. This *participate-and-reflect* mode of learning enables the resident to offer something to the ministry event without bearing the load of responsibility, which will still fall primarily on the pastor.

This mode of learning is like sitting in the co-pilot seat while flying a plane. The co-pilot has enough training to take over for the pilot in an emergency, and the pilot may give the co-pilot the opportunity to fly the plane under certain circumstances in order to spell him or simply to build the co-pilot's confidence. If, for instance, a co-pilot lands the plane on a particular flight, the pilot and co-pilot can then review how it went. They can discuss the rate of descent, the wind effects on the plane, and how the co-pilot gradually brought the plane to a stop or taxied it to the gate.

It's one thing to act, but acting without reflecting upon the action misses a learning opportunity. Reflection does not imply negative criticism: it may affirm as well as correct. Reflection makes conscious the thoughts and actions that created the ministry interaction and its outcome. Reflection helps to inculcate good habits of ministry and develops sound pastoral instinct.

Residents can participate in pastoral ministry in many ways. They can be part of worship planning, lead pastoral prayers in worship, and make hospital rounds with experienced ministers. The residency program at Wilshire caused us to reflect upon and revise our staff practice of hospital visitation. We had previously sent individual staff ministers to the hospitals to visit parishioner patients. But with residents on hand, we began to match a resident with the pastor or an associate minister. They go together now, and they are able to reflect together on each visit as they do. As the resident grows in confidence, she will take her turn leading in the pastoral visit. She will initiate conversation and say the concluding prayer. This move from *participation toward leadership* in ministry is the trajectory of good program design.

One of our recent residents accidentally experienced the value of this movement from participation toward leadership in a crisis situation. As he neared the end of his residency, we learned of the suicide of the middle-aged daughter of an elderly woman in our church. I invited the resident to meet me at the woman's house. Ordinarily we would go in together, but with all the cars of caring family and friends parked in front of the house, he mistakenly thought one of them was mine and so proceeded into the living room. Not finding me there, he suddenly knew he was being looked to as a pastor. He had been rightly trained to avoid platitudes, to sit in silence and simply bring the presence of Christ with him. But the distraught mother was asking questions that challenged his pastoral paradigm. He felt uncomfortable answering her. He felt inadequate to the task. Shortly thereafter I arrived, and he was able to listen and watch as I fielded the woman's questions, helping to direct her hope more clearly on what could be known and how faith would carry her through. The resident and I were able to huddle together by our cars afterward. He confessed his feeling of inadequacy, and I was able to affirm his instincts not to do more harm than good by answering questions that are better left to the mystery of God. Nonetheless, he was able to see that when pastors are called upon in those moments, we are called to speak words that center on the sufficiency of Christ and that help to lead the bereaved along paths of grief that will lead to comfort and healing. Upon becoming a pastor just few months later, he was able to report to me about two similar pastoral situations he found himself in. He remembered the previous experience and felt more confident and competent in his pastoral care because of it. Here's how he put it: "I have followed my instinct to be present, to listen and provide empathy in that time of confusion and sorrow. But I have also remembered your encouragement that as ministers of the Gospel, we are called to offer more than presence. We are called to offer gentle reminders of God's abiding presence. We are called to repeat the promises of God, to tenderly proclaim that healing will eventually soothe their wounded soul."

What was intended to be a participate-and-reflect mode of learning inadvertently turned into a *lead-and-reflect* occasion. This illustrates the truism that if participate-and-reflect is an appropriate mode of pastoral learning for a resident, lead-and-reflect is even more so: it most closely simulates the pastoral life. The goal is for residents to be able to perform all the duties of the pastoral office by the time they leave the program. And to do that, they must have opportunity to lead.

Because residents are generally not given specific program assignments, the normal duties of preaching and liturgical leadership, pastoral care, and administrative oversight continue to fall on the pastor and permanent staff. Churches have to find ways of making space for residents to lead. They need to preach as frequently as possible. They need to officiate at funerals, memorials, and gravesides. They need to conduct wedding ceremonies, baptize, celebrate at the Lord's Table, teach confirmation classes, and lead committee, staff, and congregational meetings, among other things. A pastoral residency program will be effective only to the degree that residents are able to move into the captain's seat. They gain their best experience by doing ministry themselves, even if mentors, peers, and the congregation attend to them by prayer and presence before, during, and after these ministry moments.

Designing the Transition Out of Residency

The established limited term of the residency has no exact parallel to the ministry life.[1] One inherent challenge to the residency process is that in the last six months or so residents become preoccupied with finding their next call. This is especially true in nonconnectional church polities, where ministers are essentially free agents in a market system of employment and congregations search for their ministers through informal networking processes. This creates anxiety for residents, who have to take great initiative to find their next place of ministry within the prescribed time.[2] But even in connectional polities that work with residents toward their next placement, residents are focused on preparing written documents, polishing résumés, and scheduling interviews.

Residency churches can help this process in various ways. During the last six months of the residency, interviews with mock search committees can be scheduled that will allow residents to practice their answers and develop their own questions for potential interview processes. Church officials and human resource professionals may help residents prepare their portfolio of résumé, sermons, and other resources. They may also consult with residents about dress and communication protocols.

Charles Street AME Church in Roxbury, Massachusetts, has developed a creative way to prepare residents for the transition. The "foundations manual" it helps each resident compile contains twelve sermons, a six-month Bible study curriculum, a new members' class curriculum, training materials for stewards and trustees, and sample budgets. The components of the manual will need to be modified to fit the church cultures of various traditions, but the idea is to carry from the residency whatever will make it easier to transition to the first call. Preparing the manual will also help residents focus on substantive matters that may be otherwise neglected in the processes of securing a call.

Finally, churches can help residents finish well by designing rituals of blessing and sending. These may be done with a special service of worship or be included as an element of Sunday worship. Just as the congregation will celebrate the coming of new residents in various ways, praying for their success and committing to their support, so also the residency church can bless these graduates of the program and send them out with commitments to continuing relationship. A framed certificate of completion of the program may be presented during the blessing ritual. Other gifts might include a pastoral robe and/or stole, biblical commentaries, and other gifts that might either remind the resident of his or her time at the church or that might be utilized in subsequent ministry calls. Wilshire has commissioned a professional potter to produce a unique chalice and paten for each graduating resident. These gifts may be presented during the ritual of blessing, along with a litany and/or prayer that might include the laying on of hands by residency program leadership.

Chapter 6

Designing the Program

STRUCTURING THE WORK OF RESIDENTS

If the last chapter addressed the need for establishing the habits and style of work that correspond to the life of ministry, there still remains the actual activities of a pastor's work and how best to structure learning them over two years of residency.

We become what we do. If residents are to become effective pastors, they will need to do the work of pastors during their residency. Some of what a pastor does she does every week, and some of what he does he does now and then. The former are therefore core competencies to be developed, while the latter, though not unimportant, are less central to the activity of a typical pastor's week. The structure of the residents' work during the residency should account for this weighting of responsibilities.

Focus on Core Competencies

Some activities are done by pastors week after week. These include preaching and worship leadership, teaching, pastoral care, and administrative duties. While it is impossible to focus intensely on each area, and while different church traditions may place greater weight on other areas, these core competencies deserve special attention.

PREACHING AND WORSHIP LEADERSHIP

The writer of the Epistle of James may be right that bringing back a soul that has wandered from the truth covers a multitude of sins (5:20), but consistently good preaching over time covers a multitude of pastoral weaknesses. Good preaching builds the life of the church in ways that nothing else can. For one thing, the largest gathering of the faithful will occur for one or more hours on Sunday mornings. Most other ministry is done individually or in small groups, but the pastor can address the whole congregation from the pulpit when preaching. Making the most of that time will strengthen the congregation spiritually and enhance the congregation's trust in the pastor as a reliable spiritual guide and leader.

Residency programs profit by giving extra weight to the development of preaching. The best way to do this is to create as many preaching opportunities for residents as possible. Frequent preaching aids the development of the young preacher.

Becoming truly proficient in any discipline may take 10,000 hours of practice.[1] Whether you are talking about flying planes or playing a violin or shooting a basketball, there's no substitute for that inexorable level of practice repetitions. This explains why most preachers come into the height of their powers in their mid-to-late forties, or after about twenty years of preaching.[2] A residency program can help establish the habits of good preaching, but the more repetitions the better.

The challenge is always in finding enough preaching times and venues to simulate the rhythm of the preaching life. Most congregations will still expect the senior pastor to preach the majority of Sunday mornings, but residents should be given as many chances to take a turn as possible. If a church has two or more weekend worship times, more than one resident may be used, thus giving more opportunities to each. Nearby churches are often looking for a guest preacher when the pastor is out. Senior living facilities and nursing homes often have chapel services where residents may preach from time to time. Church-related schools may have chapel services that need preachers. Special services throughout the year, such as Holy Week luncheons, Easter sunrise worship, and services for healing and wholeness or for the bereaved provide additional settings for resident preaching. Wilshire created a Sunday evening vespers service that is held six times a year in the chapel. The service gives residents the opportunity to preach, celebrate at the Lord's Table, and lead worship in other ways. The smaller space matches the setting of the likely church to which a resident will go next as pastor.

The benefit of creating different venues for residents to preach, apart from the normal Sunday morning worship times, is that they are able to develop a feel for a diversity of settings and styles: smaller or larger congregations, higher or lower liturgical approaches, and sometimes different mixes of generations or ethnicities. Preachers need a measure of agility in adapting their preaching style and voice to specific rooms, rites, and worshipers. It will also help them to discern where they feel most gifted to serve when they begin to consider placement toward the end of the program. Moreover, when church search committees look for a new pastor, one of the first things they ask for are sermons to view, listen to, or read.

Churches want competent preachers, and the more residents preach during their residency time, the better they will become.

Preaching benefits greatly from practice, but even more so by being a reflective practice. Weekly seminars, one-on-one work with a good preaching mentor (usually the pastor), video review of residents' sermons, and occasional special preaching events are just a few of the ways to accomplish this.

Two models that address preaching as reflective practice are the programs of the Second Presbyterian Church in Indianapolis and the Dallas Residency Cluster. Second Presbyterian continues the tradition that began with the creation of the first residency program in the mid-1990s under the leadership of the former senior minister, William Enright. Bill's successor, Lewis Galloway, hosts the residents for dinner at his home every Wednesday night. Nothing is off the table for conversation, but preaching is normally on the menu. Residents will have preached sermons that they may watch together on DVD and then discuss.

The Dallas cluster of residency churches sets aside an hour and a half every Tuesday afternoon during the fall, winter, and spring for preaching work. Residents are given assignments to prepare a sermon or lead the critique of one prepared by a peer. If a resident is going to preach on a given Sunday, the sermon is due to the entire group the prior Sunday morning. That gives the resident a sense of being ready to preach on Sunday, and it gives a week for advance feedback from the group that can be taken into account in editing the sermon for the actual preaching event. Most weeks a resident has a DVD of a recently preached sermon that allows the group to see the resident in action.

Sometimes residents preach their upcoming sermon for the group in a chapel setting. This allows for further feedback on delivery skills. Mentor pastors take turns leading these sessions and offering their wisdom and guidance, often also allowing residents to critique their work. Churches might also strengthen resident competency in preaching by bringing in excellent preaching practitioners or teachers for a special session on the craft, or they may provide the resources to send them to preaching workshops being offered around the country. One example is the preaching practicum hosted by Wilshire Baptist Church each year. We bring one preacher in from around the country, sometimes a homiletics professor at a seminary and sometimes a preaching minister in a local church. We spend a day and a half talking about preparation and delivery of the sermon in all its many facets. By keeping the group to 25 or 30 each year, there is plenty of interaction among the participants and with the leaders. Attending special conferences like these during the residency time also ingrains the practice of lifelong learning that should continue with the residents when they become pastors.

Preaching is performed in the context of worship. It is one form of liturgical leadership. Other roles of pastoral leadership in worship may include designing the services themselves, leading the prayers of the people, reading scripture, using the prayer book of a church's particular tradition, celebrating at the Lord's Table, or offering an altar call as an invitation to faith, spiritual renewal, or church membership.

Residents should be included in weekly worship preparation meetings. These meetings will allow them to participate in evaluation of worship from the previous week and help in the planning of the worship for upcoming Sundays. They might be given assignments that include enlistment and training of lay leadership or preparation of the elements such as candles, vestments, or Communion supplies. They will become familiar with the church's hymnal and learn to construct and conduct worship in a way that moves the worshipers through a service with reverence and joy. They will gain a knack for the theological and emotional flow of worship, both of which deepen the spiritual quality of the congregation's offering to God and experience of God's grace.

Teaching

Sunday school classes, Wednesday Bible study, retreats, new member orientation, confirmation classes: venues abound that call for a pastor to teach. Preaching ministry and teaching ministry are closely related. Pastors proclaim, and pastors explain.

In a time when bibical literacy has ebbed, preachers can take less knowledge of the faith for granted in their sermons. Phrases like "the problems of Job" or "as in the days of Noah" or "cast your bread upon the waters" make no immediate impact on those who aren't familiar with the stories in the biblical record from which they come. Preachers often find themselves explaining along with proclaiming, teaching as they preach. The less familiar a congregation is with the gospel, the more teaching takes the form of preaching.

But a teaching ministry is larger than a pulpit ministry and should be distinguished from it. Congregations expect their pastors to be the chief interpreters and communicators of the faith. They know they have studied the Bible and church history enough to gain advanced degrees and pass ordination exams. When they want to understand what a Bible verse means or what the idea of predestination involves, they are likely to turn to their pastor. Sometimes this teaching takes place in personal conversation, but it often happens in church classrooms or family living rooms or public forums.

Seminary theological education teaches the church's future teachers what to teach, but it ironically neglects teaching them how to teach. Pastors need to learn the differences in teaching for cognitive gain (understanding facts) and applying that learning for new ways of looking at the faith or acting upon it. When teaching a Sunday school class, for instance, is the goal only to exegete the world of the biblical text or to lead students through that text to the text of our world today? Do we teach the Bible to people or do we teach people the Bible?

An effective teaching ministry will appeal comprehensively to head, heart, and hands, so to speak, albeit not always at the same time. Pastors want their congregation to grow in knowledge and understanding, to deepen their affection for God and their commitment to the faith, and to become personally involved in God's work in the world by doing justice and loving mercy and walking humbling with their God (Micah 6:8). They want them to be wise, loving, and engaged. Self-consciously teaching these qualities will strengthen the church if the teacher teaches well.

Residents need to practice teaching. They must develop their style of teaching as much as their style of preaching. They need to become adept at different styles of teaching that fit different learning objectives: the Socratic method of questioning helps to elicit analytic skills; the lecture method allows the most amount of information to be communicated in the shortest time; and case studies, group discussion, and whiteboarding are pedagogies that teachers employ to achieve desired learning ends. Pastors will be better teachers when they have opportunities to practice different teaching methods during their residency.

Like preaching, teaching is more than conveying content to listeners; it involves the use of voice, pacing, gestures, and technology. Delivery matters at the lectern as much as at the pulpit. New technologies have added opportunities to enhance teaching. But technology is servant only when it is mastered. It can sabotage the learning moment, however, if the teacher is not facile with using PowerPoint, the chalkboard, the overhead projector, the iPad, the flip chart, the whiteboard, or the study sheet. Technology can convey the material better or it can get in the way.

Pastors who are engaging teachers will build their congregations spiritually through this skill. Residents can sharpen their teaching. One way to improve teaching is to use the same evaluation method that is used for evaluating preaching. Because these are related skills, setting aside time to discuss and evaluate teaching during a weekly preaching seminar, for example, would be one way to address it. The use of video can help residents see themselves in action. Bringing in an experienced teacher for one-on-one sessions or a seminar with the resident cohort is another ways to improve teaching.

Pastoral Care

Pastors attend to the spiritual needs of the congregation in many ways. We are not medical doctors, but we are often called to be at the bedside when someone is ill. We are not psychologists, but we are often found attending to social and emotional matters with individuals and families. Our work is the care of souls, but since souls are always embodied we find ourselves appropriately caring for the whole person. How to do this well can be learned during a residency program. Like preaching and worship leadership, it will need weekly attention.

Residents will learn best by doing the work of the pastor in hospital visitation, homebound care, counseling with those who require spiritual guidance, and leading or participating as often as possible in services with the families of a deceased person. If possible, residents should be assigned regular pastoral visitation responsibilities. All the better if they are matched with more experienced ministers as they do so.

As with preaching and worship, special attention to pastoral care training is crucial. One way to cover this is by a regular pastoral care seminar or conversation with a trained pastor or chaplain. Chaplains can be very helpful. They are usually trained in Clinical Pastoral Education programs that pay particular attention to self-awareness in the pastoral setting, sensitivity to the person who is experiencing the illness or grief rather than focusing on the illness or grief itself, as well as the many nuances of navigating a visit that might include deference to hospital staff and patient's families, or how to pray with or for the infirm based on the particular circumstance the pastor finds. What becomes second nature to an experienced pastor comes at first to a resident as an unknown challenge. Seminary can only provide classroom case studies that are one or two steps removed from the actual experience of pastoral care. Residencies allow for reflective practice on these important pastoral duties.

Likewise, pastors develop bonds with their congregations over time by their work in life-cycle faith events such as child dedications and baptisms, weddings, and funerals or memorial services. Leading well in these moments builds a wealth of spiritual capital for pastors. But these occasions are often fraught with high emotions and expectations that require pastoral wisdom. For instance, when a couple is planning to marry, they are often dealing with family tensions that come out in the planning of the event. Pastors need to be able to do more than lay out the church's policies on how weddings are conducted; they need to conduct the couple as they walk through the many potential minefields of family dynamics that can sabotage any marriage. Or in the case of memorial services, helping the families walk through their grief appropriately can be challenging in the midst of raw emotion. Many families would rather only celebrate the life of the deceased, because the pain of the loss is too great to address. But the church cannot capitulate to a death-denying culture. It has to celebrate life as a gift of God that includes the reality of death. Pastors need to guide families through this process by saying no at times to liturgical options the family might request that would undermine the spiritual nature of worship in favor of something more like a testimonial to the goodness of the deceased. This takes pastoral aplomb. While reflective practice is the best means of learning, reading books or articles together on the subject, and reflecting upon them together, can help.

Eugene Petersen writes with incomparable deftness about the pastoral life. Reading his books or articles together can benefit residents greatly. One example is a piece he wrote about being the pastor of a recovering addict.[3] He reflects upon why it has always been difficult for him to be an effective pastor to alcoholics, because of his own family experience with an alcoholic father. Reading about this can stimulate reflection on how a pastor's family of origin might shape encounters with people dealing with related matters in their own lives. But beyond that, Petersen describes how he helped a recovering cocaine addict, who had become a Christian, make his wedding a more formative Christian event. The man and his fiancée were unschooled in Christian hymnody but enjoyed country music. They requested that an Emmylou Harris song be sung in the wedding. Eugene understood their sentiment, but he also knew that his pastoral duty was more than and higher than a mere celebration of human love. So he suggested "something more in keeping with the new life they were now living" as Christians. They agreed to his suggestion of what Petersen thought of as a country-sounding Christian favorite, "Farther Along." That song became a theme for the man's Christian experience from that day forward, but only because an experienced pastor knew how to execute a nudge toward the holy.

Skilled pastors are holy nudgers. They don't push and shove. They don't slink and back away. They nudge people gracefully toward more sublime experiences of the divine. Residents will make better pastors if they have practiced the art of such purposeful persuasion.

Most churches that host residency programs utilize regular seminar times to reflect on the pastoral life. They read and reflect on the theology of pastoral practice with the senior pastor or designated mentor. They discuss recent pastoral experiences that have occurred in the life of the church. They may also report and reflect with the program coordinator about their own pastoral experiences in one-to-one conversation settings. Once again, the point is to use a variety of learning modes to sharpen resident skills and expand pastoral imagination.

ADMINISTRATIVE LEADERSHIP

Louis Weeks calls it "scutwork." Most pastors would sooner scuttle scutwork than do it. It's the nitty-gritty pastoral work of seeing to it that the little things are being done effectively to achieve the church's mission. In his book, *All for God's Glory: Redeeming Church Scutwork,* Weeks puts it this way:

> Church administration is exceedingly complex. It consists of obvious tasks: making and keeping budgets; planning and assessing programs and activities; organizing worship and work efforts; enlisting officers, teachers, and staff, as well as dismissing those who cannot effectively carry out their responsibilities. But it also consists of subtle and systematic perspectives, for good planning makes for excellent worship and nurture; mission and witness are inextricable from effective organization; [and] deep, trusting partnerships among pastor, staff, and lay leadership are built on keeping promises and meeting responsibilities.[4]

These daily, weekly, and seasonal routines can make or break a pastor's ministry. Pastors don't have to do them all by themselves; they can delegate to associate staff or lay leadership. But even delegating the work to the right people requires a pastor's knowledge of the work to be done, how it is to be done, and what metric will be used to measure whether it is being done well. The residency is an ideal time to give a young pastor a thorough education in the work of church administration.

While the distinction can be overstated, most young pastors need to learn to distinguish between leadership and management. In short, leaders articulate vision and work strategically to achieve that vision. Managers organize people and resources to implement the plans of the church that the leader or leaders have envisioned. As Weeks puts it, leadership is about "marshalling resources for adaptation," and management is about "making sure resources are in place to accomplish the desired outcomes." Good leadership flows into good management, and vice versa. "That means letters written, budgets met, meetings attended, and people gaining competence and confidence all come from good management and allow for successful leadership."[5]

In smaller churches, pastors may need to manage much of the process of church administration. Even then they cannot neglect the crucial pastoral role of leadership. Leaders inspire. Leaders inspire others to do more than they might have imagined themselves. They inspire excellence in carrying out every task. They inspire loyalty to one another and fidelity to the common mission. Leaders do not have to be detail-oriented themselves, although they can be. They must, however, be aware of how things are working and whether things are working. And in order for that to be true, they need to have a working knowledge of the administrative work of the church.

In addition to pastors and program coordinators, church business administrators, human resources staffers, and financial assistants may be valuable to resident administrative formation. Residents need to learn church governance, personnel management, program coordination, communications, and financial stewardship. Rather than a weekly seminar on the subject, residents might schedule time with appropriate staff members to ask questions and learn how the church handles these matters. They may also sit in on budget development meetings, be asked to preach a sermon on stewardship, or be assigned to a committee and be asked to work with a lay chairperson in setting an agenda for a meeting and seeing it through. Residents might be allowed to moderate a church conference, if that fits within the polity of the church. They should attend governance meetings, such as vestry, church council, session, or deacons' meetings.

One way to give residents administrative experience is to assign them the work of another staff member who is on vacation, at a conference, or on sabbatical. The resident may move into that staff member's office and assume all the duties of that minister, thus learning on the job. If that minister has an administrative assistant, he or she can be helpful in guiding the resident through the work.

Most young pastors are surprised to learn how much writing a pastor does. Sermons, letters, email, Web pages, newsletter columns, and occasional congregational letters are just a few of the kinds of writing regularly required of a pastor. Senior pastors may share the writing of their newsletter columns with residents, giving young pastors practice in thinking about how to write for the spiritual nurture of the congregation. English teachers, journalists, and creative writing experts may be brought in for a one-time workshop or expense money can be provided for residents to attend a writing seminar.

Central Presbyterian Church in Atlanta is a downtown church with a metropolitan constituency. It has created a nine-parish system that is geographically based. Each of their three residents is assigned pastoral responsibilities for two parishes. They not only get to attend to the pastoral care of their parishes, they help to coordinate life within the parishes. This involves periodic fellowship gatherings, communication, and mission activities. Any pastoral leadership opportunities that can be given to residents will strengthen their hand as they learn by doing.

Similarly, many resident churches make it a staple of their programs to assign residents to initiate, organize, and lead a mission trip or local activity. Seeing to the detail work of such an enterprise gives residents experience and confidence as they move toward their first pastoral call.

A Checklist for Ministry Leadership

While the residency will focus primarily on developing the core competencies above, there are numerous rituals or events that residents need to practice at least once during their residency in order to be better prepared when they become senior pastors.

Residents may work with their program coordinator to develop a personal checklist of these activities and then take initiative in seeing to it that they accomplish these during their residency time. Items on this list might include:

- talk with a child about faith;
- handle a benevolence case;
- perform a baptism;
- lead a staff meeting;
- write a pastor's column;
- celebrate Communion;

- visit a homebound member;
- officiate at a graveside service;
- conduct a wedding;
- plan a worship service;
- organize and lead a mission trip or activity;
- speak at summer children's or youth camp;
- teach each generation in a Sunday school class;
- initiate a new ministry that will continue beyond the residency;
- learn to read a financial balance sheet;
- create and conduct a special congregational Bible or book study;
- serve in a preschool room during worship;
- interview a community organizer;
- consult with a financial professional about personal money management and retirement planning.

These are just a few of the areas of learning that do not require ongoing investment, but should be addressed during the residency in order to round out the experience.

Structuring the Work: Rotational and Immersion Approaches

There is more than one way to structure the work of residents to accomplish the goal of comprehensive pastoral leadership practice.

St. James' Episcopal Church in New York City typifies one model. They address several strands of learning by combining regular ministry, rotational focuses, and individual supervision. Residents lead in worship, preaching, and pastoral visitation weekly. Then they move through four rotations over the course of the residency that give special attention to education (the teaching ministry of the church across all ages), congregational life (fellowship activities, newcomer welcome, new member assimilation, and lay ministry support), mission (local, national, and international mission activities and partners), and parish systems (governance, stewardship, business practices, and building maintenance oversight). They work with staff and lay leaders in these specialized areas of ministry for a period of several months before moving on to another area. Throughout the residency they meet weekly with the program administrator and monthly with the rector. The weekly meetings allow them to reflect quickly on what they are doing. The monthly meetings provide a forum to ask the rector anything they wish, but that time is often used to review their preaching efforts.

A total immersion model can be found at St. Paul's Lutheran Church in Davenport, Iowa. The advantage of this nonrotational model is that it gets the residents into the rhythm of the pastoral life more quickly. Pastors don't get to focus on areas of ministry like education, stewardship, governance, or mission in designated blocks of time. Instead, they are allowed to intrude on the normal flow of pastoral life, even if they aren't part of the weekly flow of preaching, worship and pastoral care. As the St. Paul's program administrator Tammy Hermanson puts it, "The merits of an immersion model are that it provides a wide array of learning opportunities for young pastors and perhaps give them a more realistic idea of how they will need to devote their time, energies, and attention to diverse ministry responsibilities and demands in future parish settings."[6]

St. Paul's total immersion model addresses the matters St. James' covers rotationally in two ways: (1) ongoing learning goals are set by the residents and the program administrator and (2) a weekly pastoral seminar is led by the senior pastor, Peter Marty. The seminar features readings in areas such as the pastoral life, theology, leading congregational meetings, effective teaching techniques, stewardship, biblical hospitality, and writing. St. Paul's also creates periodic field trips and special seminars with guest teachers to round out the learning.

Other programs adopt aspects of each of these models in ways that seem to fit their congregational culture, their clergy styles, and their leadership expertise. Whether you design your program with or without rotations, featuring weekly or monthly seminars or some other approach, every program will want to help residents become acquainted with the rhythm of weekly work that pastors experience and find ways to address more occasional duties that round out the life of pastoral ministry.

Chapter 7

Prodding Progress

USING FEEDBACK TOOLS FOR IMPROVEMENT

"Anything worth doing is worth doing well." A pastoral residency program is worth doing, and it's worth doing well. But how do we know whether it's doing its work well?

The challenge of assessment cuts across many disciplines, including church work. The teaching profession, for instance, struggles with how to judge whether a teacher is doing a good job or not. Do you judge only outcomes? And if you judge outcomes, do you take into consideration a class's learning aptitude and where each student began and ended? Do you factor in the level of resources, such as family education and encouragement, school supplies, tutors and teacher aides, library, nutrition, and English language skill? Should teacher assessment measure whether she helped students learn how to think or only what to think?

James Howell, Senior Minister of the Myers Park United Methodist Church in Charlotte, North Carolina, acknowledges that clergy and laity alike suffer from what he terms "evaluation anxiety."[1] Everyone knows we need to do it, but no one is sure exactly how. From the clergy side alone, he argues, "the kinds of people who raise their hand to become pastors aren't fond of [typical evaluation] instruments—to put it bluntly. We do want feedback, and we really crave support. We want to cultivate stellar ministry habits. But what's the best way to do this?"

Ministry performance evaluation can be co-opted by cultural values that don't fit the spiritual aims of the church. Is a minister doing well if everyone likes her, or does that means she is a "people pleaser" who is neglecting a prophetic role in her work? If the church is doing well in attendance and donations, does that mean the pastor is effective and faithful, or could he be succumbing to business or entertainment approaches that undermine the core convictions of the faith in order to achieve worldly signs of success?

These caveats notwithstanding, when residents leave the program, we want them to be prepared to be effective pastors in their next churches. We therefore want to make sure that the program is working effectively to that end. While no evaluation tool is perfect, some process for continual improvement should be in place. Quality performance experts like to say that you can only improve what you can measure. Excellence in ministry may be metrically elusive, but efforts to prod progress in residents and programs alike will increase the odds of positive results. Making those efforts will also reinforce, in both young ministers and in the church, the commitment to continual improvement that should be a hallmark of pastors and congregations.

The good news is that churches that have done this work for nearly a decade have learned and improved by use of formal and informal feedback tools. But progress, not perfection, is the aim, as church consultant Kennon Callahan has put it: "Striving for excellence in life is a worthy goal, but perfection is impossible."² The same is true for ministry. Perfectionism can, in fact, undermine progress by creating ideals that are impossible for sinful and flawed human beings to achieve. Which is why G. K. Chesterton wittily countered the opening adage with his own: "Anything worth doing is worth doing poorly." With that realism granted, aiming for good ministry over poor is still desirable.

A pastoral residency program provides a collegial setting for aspiring young ministers to come and go, taking with them when they leave a level of proficiency owed to their time as residents. Church leaders employ various techniques to help them improve their skills. They give important feedback to residents at a formative time in their career that will shape them throughout their ministries and especially help them make a smooth and successful transition to their first call. The residency program itself also needs feedback in order for it to improve over time. Feedback may come in formal and informal ways: through tools designed to elicit specific information that can encourage and challenge, and through conversations that prod progress. These often work together to produce the best results.

Ways to Prod Progress in Residents

Ongoing Informal Feedback

Patterns develop for residents to receive feedback. Daily, they interact with congregants, staff, and each other. Periodically, they meet with their lay support team and the program administrator. Along the way, there are countless opportunities for residents to receive feedback about their performance of ministry and how others are perceiving them. Maximizing these occasions for affirmation and correction are crucial to the development of the residents. Informal nudging will help residents avoid the harsh criticism that might otherwise come in formal evaluations. It is like making small adjustments at the wheel when driving a car. Better to adjust all along the way than to wait until the car is about to go off the road and then have to jerk the wheel to get back on track.

Leaders and peers need to be deliberate in their feedback in timely ways. Wisdom will dictate when to say what. For example, giving criticism to a resident in the narthex just after she preached a sermon will not build her confidence. On the other hand, a resident will benefit from any affirmation that can be delivered soon after preaching. When a young person has done her best to deliver a message (or celebrate Communion, or lead a meeting), genuine encouragement will strengthen the resident's sense that God has used her in that offering to God and the congregation. Criticism should be postponed, however, so that the resident can have some emotional distance from the effort and the one offering feedback can decide how best to frame and phrase the criticism.

Informal feedback can take place in a brief hallway conversation, in a phone call or email, or in a one-on-one meeting. An important ingredient in any feedback is clarity about what is most important for the resident to work on at any given time. Comprehensive criticism can be overwhelming, but suggestions about one or two things to work on can yield great improvement.

In golf, good teaching professionals understand the basics of the golf swing, and they also know that some things matter more than others. Every swing is unique to some degree, but every effective swing has common elements in it. Teaching pros don't point out every flaw in a student's swing at once. They address what they see as most important first and then build from there. They also read the temperament of the student in order to discern how much instruction the student can handle at the time.

Similarly, good ministry feedback affirms what the resident is doing well and then suggests one or two things that can be worked on that will prod progress for that individual rather than impede it. The feedback can become pickier as the resident improves, because the task will move from building skills to polishing them.

Senior pastors are especially important in the informal feedback process. Because residents are preparing to do the work of senior pastors, the feedback of the one already doing that work is most salient. Residents consistently cite the relationship with the senior pastor as a major factor in the quality of the residency experience. Senior pastors prod progress in residents as they develop relationships of trust through gestures of time and attention. Small moments of encouragement can be matched with larger moments of intentional consultation. Both modes of feedback are important, and they will mutually reinforce each other.

Senior pastors function a bit like the leader of a band. Art Blakey was the leader and drummer for a combo known as the Jazz Messengers. Blakey kept time with two fists. But he did more than maintain the band's rhythm; he nudged every player to become his best. As one commentator put it:

As the leader of the perpetually changing Jazz Messengers, Art fostered generations of new players, many of whom went on to become formidable leaders themselves. It was the school of real knocks, the boot camp from which one emerged a hardened, swinging individual. As much as Blakey's drumming style is immortal, his generous nurturing of jazz's future, via bandstand training, stands equal in importance.[3]

In a 1988 documentary, Blakey talked about how a combo works and what he did to make it work. He saw himself as the teacher who mentored his jazz students by altering his drumming to challenge or encourage each soloist. In typical jazz performance, the spotlight moves from one player to another, from the pianist to the bassist to the trumpeter, and so on. Blakey would sit behind the drums and evaluate how each player was doing. If the soloist was playing well, he would simply keep the beat and let the light shine on the individual. But if the soloist was underperforming in Blakey's estimation, he would pick up his drumming—getting louder and stronger—to let the featured player know he had to do better. If the player improved, Blakey would back off. If not, he would move the solo to another player.

This informal approach to prodding progress in the process of doing ministry can make formal evaluation easier, because the issues are already raised in the course of doing the work. And yet, the analogy can be pushed too far if it seems that only the senior pastor or supervisor is responsible for prodding progress or only informal feedback is helpful. Other leaders can also advance the cause of resident improvement. The program administrator can make sure that residents are fulfilling their learning plans through periodic consultation.

Peers can point out how residents are working with them collegially. They can give feedback on sermons and other ministry practices. Key lay people can do the same.

For example, a member of a lay support team took one of our residents to lunch to discuss his skill at conducting a meeting. Residents work with the chair of the lay support team to develop agendas and conduct meetings. This partnership is somewhat like a dance in which one leads and the other follows. But if a meeting seems to go off course, the resident needs to learn how to not step on the chair's toes and lead without seeming to take over. The layman, whose professional life depends on conducting and participating in effective meetings, gave the resident tips on how to step in, when to step back, and how to make sure the agenda is completed successfully.

SHARED MINISTRY PLANS

Residents will grow best when they are clear about their direction. They should be able to contribute to their own learning plan, since one great benefit of this process is that they develop habits of self-evaluation that will serve them well in the years ahead. Many churches use a collaborative process to develop a learning plan. Sometimes this forms the basis for more formal evaluation. Sometimes this takes the form of an individualized learning plan that includes specific areas of competence building, such as preaching, preparing a budget, or leading a staff meeting. Sometimes it involves areas of needed growth based on the resident's own awareness or in response to the assessment of others.

The Making Excellent Disciples program of the Episcopal Diocese of Chicago requires residents to develop a Ministry

Action Plan that focuses on the twelve clergy competencies listed in Jill M. Hudson's book *When Better Isn't Enough: Evaluation Tools for the 21st Century Church.*[4] These include such characteristics as the ability to maintain personal, professional, and spiritual balance; guiding conversion experiences; evangelism; vision casting; leading change; developing lay leaders; managing conflict; and being a lifelong learner, among others. The resident and key leaders address questions about what was planned and what was accomplished during the period in question and what remains to be done. The resident gives a self-assessment to the group followed by assessments of the resident by those present. The goal is coaching more than criticism, encouragement more than blaming. They operate under the assumption that 20 percent of a minister's work gets 80 percent of the results. This helps residents focus on those aspects of ministry that will have the greatest impact on the congregation. Young ministers are overwhelmed with the multiplicity of tasks that go into parish ministry. They have trouble prioritizing. The feedback of these reviews helps residents distinguish between what is most important and what seems most urgent.

Some congregations employ evaluation tools that correspond to the method of permanent staff review. The benefits of this system are that it creates a sense that residents are a part of the full staff and not treated differently, and it also helps to introduce residents to a process they may wish to adopt when they are pastors.

Any shared ministry plan should take account of progress in the core competencies of preaching and worship leadership, teaching, pastoral care, and administration. While the sum is always greater than the parts, these areas hold great weight in making up the whole of a pastor's skill set. And yet, they may not get at all the intangibles that round out a pastor's relationships with peer colleagues and the congregation. Another tool, like a 360-degree evaluation instrument, described below, might supplement the process.

THE 360-DEGREE EVALUATION

A 360-degree evaluation is a process that provides feedback from all vantage points around the subject, including that of the subject of the evaluation. The Transition into Ministry community has developed and shared a 360-degree evaluation designed specifically for transition into ministry programs. Wilshire has adapted it for our own context.[5] Other churches have done the same. This evaluation features questions that get at more than skills. They address the bearing of the minister, her sense of pastoral identity, and how he is experienced by others. It allows reviewers to mark the resident somewhere on a continuum between extremes—either of which would be undesirable in effective pastoral ministry. It also allows for written comments for each question.

The concept of a 360-degree evaluation derives from the assumption that we are all being evaluated at all times from all directions in the congregational system. Supervisors, subordinates, and peers all get a say, both clergy and lay. The resident fills one out on himself first, and then the anonymous assessments of others are collated and compared to the resident's self-evaluation. The resident is given some time to read and process the evaluation alone. Then the senior pastor and program administrator will sit down and discuss the evaluation with the resident. The consultation will give the supervisors the opportunity to reinforce particular areas of needed emphasis. It may also allow them to interpret the feedback in constructive ways. Sometimes things written anonymously can be cold data that stings. The care of pastoral leaders in these moments helps the medicine go down.

Sometimes these evaluations awaken residents to things they could not otherwise face up to in themselves. In one case at Wilshire, it became the basis for the mutual decision to discontinue the residency. The lack of promise the evaluation pointed to made clear that the investment of the resident and the church over the eighteen-month balance of the residency would not be worthwhile. In a 24-month residency, these 360-degree assessments might be undertaken twice—at the 6 and 18-month points, the first one providing a benchmark from which to measure progress on the second.[6]

Plymouth Congregational Church in Des Moines devised its own survey using the online resource Survey Monkey. They sent it to members of the congregation to receive feedback beyond the scope of those most closely involved in the program. This 360-like approach can yield important feedback that might otherwise be missed. In the case of one Plymouth resident, reading the survey results forced her to acknowledge something in her demeanor with the congregation that she knew she had to change but might not have addressed without the feedback coming in that form.

APPRECIATIVE INQUIRY

Another approach to assessment is to use a process known as appreciative inquiry. This approach focuses more on possibilities than problems; it views the person and the system together in such a way as to seek improvement in both at the same time. It uses leading questions that allow the resident to reflect upon and articulate how he sees his progress and where the program operates at its best, such as these:

- "What am I (the resident) doing well?"
- "What are we (the church residency program) doing well?"
- "What am I troubled by?"
- "What value does the program need to reassert?"

By including the resident in the process of making herself and the program better at the same time, a collaborative spirit of improvement minimizes competitive, combative, or conflictual feelings about the evaluation process.[7]

Assessing the Residency Program

It's one thing to prod progress in individual residents; it's another thing to keep making changes to the program itself to serve that end. No program is infallible. None is beyond improvement. Like residents who are always works in process, the program itself needs to make adjustments along the way in order to be effective. Mentors need to know whether their mentoring style is producing desired results. The curriculum design may need alteration if it is more work about the work rather than the work itself. Lay support teams may need better training or direction. The recruiting process may need to be tweaked in order to make better decisions about candidates. The Pastoral Residency Oversight Committee will want the best information possible that will allow it to hone the impact of the program for long-term success.

Resident Evaluations of the Program

The residents themselves have a vantage point unlike any other from which to assess the program. Soliciting their feedback reinforces their partnership in the program's success. It helps them move away from a "student" mindset to a "professional" one.

As with the 360-degree evaluation tool for residents, the TiM community has developed three instruments to help residents assess the program at the beginning, middle, and ending of their time at the church.[8] On their own, each of these evaluations give leaders snapshots of the program at different points in time; together, they demonstrate the effects of the adjustments the program has made along the way.

- Entrance Evaluation: The first instrument attempts to take a sounding of the new resident's expectations of the program as she enters it. Program leaders will be able to judge how well they communicated with the resident during the recruitment process and time of assimilation into the congregation.

- Mid-point Evaluation: The transition from first year to second year is a revealing turning point. Most residents take a noticeable step forward in their confidence at this juncture. The effect is almost like a time-release capsule that has been releasing medicine into the bloodstream over time. Residents often speak more assertively and authoritatively about their experience, having crossed the bridge from newcomers to program veterans. Their insights into the program at this point allows time to make adjustments if needed for the crucial second year ahead.

• Exit Evaluation: The final piece completes the residents' perspectives on the two-year experience. Has the program succeeded in fulfilling the hopes the residents brought into it? What could have been done differently or better? Do they feel ready to move into pastoral positions as the program promised?

Churches that have evaluated their program over time have made numerous changes to improve them. St. Paul's Lutheran Church in Davenport, Iowa, changed from a rotational model to an immersion model that fit their context better. Central Presbyterian Church in Atlanta altered their class and term configuration to have one new resident enter and leave each year on a three year basis. As described earlier, they also assigned residents to a geographical parish for the duration of their service in order to give them a greater sense of being the pastor to a particular group of people. Wellesley Congregational Church moved from a staggered class of residents to a unified cohort: two residents entering and leaving the program together. And Wilshire has modified its rotational model, creating a hybrid form of immersion and rotation. The only two rotations residents now go through are discipleship/education ministries in the first year and stewardship/administrative ministries in the second year. Giving each of those a year-long focus has proven better than the previous model in which they were only given three months each.

Longitudinal Assessment

We call this work "transition into ministry." We do everything we think is necessary to help residents make a good transition into their first full time permanent staff position. But are we succeeding?

Those who have graduated from the program will have more perspective over time about the program's effectiveness. Churches should seek input from former residents from time to time on how the program looks to them from the horizon of one or more years out. This can be done by phone, at a reunion of residents hosted by the church, by use of online resources like Survey Monkey, through an established communication channel set up with resident alumni such as a closed Facebook group, or by letter or email survey.

Possible queries might include: How did the first year go in your new church? In what ways did the program prepare you well for pastoral ministry? What areas could the program better address to strengthen your first year or your first three to five years? Are we missing something? How can the residency church continue to have a constructive role in your ongoing ministry?

Deciding When to Pause or Stop

Most churches have an easier time starting something new than stopping something old. Once a program gets underway, it's difficult to discontinue it. It feels like failure to admit the time to end the effort has come. A pastoral residency program may start with much energy and excitement. It may garner broad support from the congregation. Yet, if the conditions that made it possible have changed, continuing the program may do more harm than good for the church and residents.

Assessing the program from time to time and making the decision to continue it, change it, pause it, or end it will only build more credibility with the congregation. But how might that decision be reached, and what questions might be asked to discern the way? The Pastoral Residency Oversight Committee (or its equal in the congregational structure of the church) should assess the program annually by a means already mentioned or another of its own design. It should ask whether the church is actually becoming a teaching congregation, thus fulfilling the cultural mandate for a successful residency. It should take stock of the leadership team and ask whether all the necessary mentors are still in place and functioning well. When a senior pastor who has loved the mentoring role leaves the church for one reason or another, that will handicap the program. It may be prudent to take a hiatus for a year or two until a new pastor is in place and the program can be restarted.

Similarly, if resident recruitment is unsuccessful in a given year, or the quality of candidates is not up to expectations, a pause may be called for. St. Paul's Lutheran Church in Davenport had just that experience. It allowed them a year to step back and take stock of how the program was conducted, something they might not have had the time or perspective to do if they had welcomed a new resident cohort.

Financial capacity is crucial to determining whether to continue the program. If economic hardship hits the church and program resources are depleted, it may be best to take time to regroup. If the church undergoes considerable conflict over some matter of denominational decision, doctrinal dispute, or leadership crisis, the capacity to sustain a healthy environment for a residency program will be impaired. Residents can learn a great deal by walking with congregations through challenging times, but if the fellowship becomes toxic, it may be best to suspend the program rather than discourage residents about the life of the church at such a formative time.

Chapter 8

Building Capital

SECURING THE FUNDS TO
START AND SUSTAIN A PROGRAM

Every new business venture starts with great enthusiasm, but many soon fail. The U.S. Small Business Administration reports that three out of ten new businesses fail within two years, and only half survive five years. Experts cite numerous reasons for business failure including planning, location, staffing, and sales. But most reasons can be boiled down to two: poor management skills and lack of capitalization.

Starting and sustaining a successful church-based pastoral residency program similarly requires good management and adequate funding. Much of what we have said so far addresses the former. We have looked at a vision for the work, the design of the program, the personnel needed to operate it, and ways to nurture the culture of the congregation to make it most effective. What remains is the money needed to begin and to keep going for the long term.

The two-stage process of locating startup funds and then developing the long-term resources actually requires one prior step: developing a realistic estimate of the costs of conducting a residency program.

Developing a Projected Budget and Business Plan

The Gospel of Luke records that Jesus told a parable in which he compared the cost of following him to a construction project. "For which of you, intending to build a tower, does not first sit down and estimate the cost, to see whether he has enough to complete it? Otherwise, when he has laid a foundation and is not able to finish, all who see it will begin to ridicule him, saying, 'This fellow began to build and was not able to finish'" (14:28–30). It's one thing to begin a residency program; it's another to be able to continue it over time. Estimating the costs of establishing and sustaining a program will prevent the embarrassment of a well-intended but short-lived venture. A budget should be developed before beginning a program that corresponds to the term of the first resident or residents, either two years or three.[1] A business plan that projects income as well as expenses over that time will round out the projection.

Salary and Benefits

A resident should be paid enough to merit the position but not so much that moving to a first call after the residency would be a step backward. Determining a reasonable compensation package might depend upon the relative salary structure of the permanent staff and the cost of living in the area where the church is located. One way to compute this would be to pay at a level commensurate with an entry-level permanent staff member. Another comparison would be the pay of a starting teacher salary in local public schools or that of nonprofit professional positions in the community. As a general rule, a salary somewhere between $35,000–$45,000 per year (including housing allowance) is typical. That number might be more toward the lower or the higher end depending upon the cost of housing.

Churches should pay health insurance for residents in keeping with the pattern of benefits provided to permanent staff. If the church pays full or partial premiums for permanent staff, it should do so for residents. If the church pays for dependent coverage of permanent staff, it should do so for residents also. It's important to treat residents as staff colleagues, not as student interns. Some denominations require that all ministers be enrolled in their benefits plan, which takes away decision-making on the matter. That may include retirement contributions as well. Since the resident's age, marital status, and number of dependents will vary, the church might add 30 percent or more to salary to arrive at a round number estimate for planning purposes.

OFFICE SETUP

The church should provide the resident with a computer, preferably a portable laptop. Office space with desk, phone, and supplies will add to the cost. The first year will be more expensive, but the cost of office expenses should be about $1,500 annually.

PROGRAM EXPENSES

A book and periodicals allowance might run about $300 per year. A convention and conference budget that would provide funds for the resident to attend denominational meetings and professional enrichment conferences will make possible additional networking and learning opportunities. Another $1,000 minimum should be budgeted for travel, lodging, meals and fees.

RECRUITMENT AND MOVING EXPENSES

When a church recruits a resident, it will need to plan for the cost of recruitment. This may involve the cost for the senior pastor or other designated church official to visit a seminary. It will certainly include at least one trip for more than one candidate to visit the church for interviews. It will likely include a second visit of the resident (or residents) who has been called and who has accepted the position to find housing. These costs may run several thousand dollars, depending upon the number of trips and the distance traveled. Figure on $2,000 minimum for the first year only.

Reasonable moving expenses should be budgeted also. Even if the residency is just a two-year stint, the church should treat the resident as a qualified minister who is coming to serve the congregation. Since churches typically pay moving expenses for new permanent staff, they should do so also for residents. Moving costs can vary greatly depending upon whether a professional mover is employed, how much packing the resident does, and how far the resident is traveling. Reasonable costs might be about $2,500.

ADMINISTRATIVE PERSONNEL

Although a church may simply add administrative oversight to the work of existing personnel, it may need to increase the pay of an administrator or hire a part-time person to oversee the program. This will be difficult to estimate, because it will depend entirely upon how the church constructs its program, but these costs must be included in any estimate.

The Business Plan

A goal without a plan is just a wish. Based upon the initial budget developed for the program, a spreadsheet may be produced that projects costs over several years under categories such as personnel (salary and benefits), administration (office, computers, etc.), recruitment, other program expenses (meetings, conferences, etc.), and a contingency fund. Expected costs should be matched by projected revenue. For instance, if the church receives startup funds from a grant or one-time donation, it needs to account for replacement of those funds in future years. The church may begin to build savings into its budget right away that will soften the blow in future years when the church has to pick up more of the cost of the program. These ideas are discussed in more detail below, but the key is to project income as well as expenses over a designated period that should cover at least one resident term.

One way to go about estimating costs is to request budgets from churches that conduct residency programs and then estimate your own costs off of those numbers. However you arrive at a budget, be sure you have estimated high enough, even if you add additional contingency funds to cover unexpected expenses. When seeking startup funds—whether from the church's own ministry fund or from other sources, having a sound estimate of the costs will strengthen the case and build credibility with funders.

Locating Startup Funds

Churches may want to begin a residency program, may believe they have the congregational culture and key leaders to make it work, and yet still have a difficult time finding the initial financial resources to fund it. We have already discussed the cost-effectiveness of converting an existing permanent staff position into a residency. This approach will minimize the need for additional funds, but it will not eliminate that need altogether. For instance, recruiting and moving costs will have to be budgeted every two or three years rather than once for a permanent staff member.[2] Office setup costs will also be higher due to the more frequent turnover of residents than permanent staff ministers.

If the church decides to add one or more residents who need new funding, the challenge to the congregation may be too steep to move forward without securing startup funds that will help establish the program and give the church time to build financial capacity to sustain it. Potential donors sometimes have a difficult time understanding a residency in theory. When they see it in action and realize its continuing value to the church and its mission, they are more likely to give to sustain it. But getting off to a good start is crucial. Ideally, a horizon of three to five years of funding will give the church the best chance of building the capital necessary to self-fund the venture. A church might safely aim to have funds in place to cover the full cost of one residency term— whether two years or three—for however many residents it calls.

Depending upon the amount the church is able to allocate to the program, some or all of the startup costs may be need to be sought from various sources. The church may, for example, have the money to provide the compensation costs for the resident(s) but need help with program or logistical costs—or vice versa. Sharing the cost between the congregation and a funder will give all parties a greater sense of investment in the program. With that in mind, four possible sources for initial funding should be considered: individuals, denominations and judicatories, seminaries, and foundations.

INDIVIDUALS

A congregation may have a member who possesses the personal resources to provide startup money for a residency program. This is the model that helped to begin the original program at Second Presbyterian Church in Indianapolis. Visionary church members, Tom and Marjorie Lake, believed in the idea and provided an initial gift to help pilot the program. Once the program was well established, they gave addition funds to endow it in perpetuity. The Lake Fellows, as their residents are known, have proven the wisdom of that generous act.

Senior pastors generally know best whom to approach with this idea, and they are usually the best ones to make the "ask." Sometimes these individuals are known to have long-established high net worth, but sometimes an individual may have had a recent "liquidity event," such as the sale of a business or property that may leave the person with tax consequences that might be minimized with a significant charitable gift in the same year. People with wealth in the church often look for opportunities to do something spiritually significant with their material blessings. You can count on their being approached by philanthropic arts, health, and educational organizations for generous donations. The church should see itself as a prime candidate for helping potential donors act on their desire to be good stewards of God's gifts. Funding at least the cost of starting a residency program in their church might appeal to their love for God and their concern for the future of the church's leadership. What's more, if they make an initial gift, they may be candidates to help sustain the program in the long term. Other wealthy people in the community, known to be passionate about their faith but members of another congregation, might also be appealed to for startup funds.

DENOMINATIONS AND JUDICATORIES

Denominations have a pressing need for well-trained young clergy. They may have taken note of the effect of pastoral residencies in producing well-prepared pastors for congregations. Some have invested in creative approaches to spur residencies or residency-like programs in their congregations. Churches interested in hosting a residency program should approach national or local denominational bodies to see what funding partnerships might be available.

In some cases, anchor churches that have run residency programs of their own have expanded their reach by creating larger partnerships with local churches and judicatories. As previously mentioned, the Massachusetts Conference of the United Church of Christ has done something like this as a result of the work of the Village Church in Wellesley.

Christ Episcopal Church in Alexandria, Virginia, has done something similar, using a residency model. They have created a Washington area program that requires churches to contribute resources of their own for resident compensation and have formed a nonprofit organization that raises additional funds to support the work. A foundation adds program costs to round out the funding.

Two local synods of the Evangelical Lutheran Church in America have contributed from line items in their budgets for first-call pastors to the residency program of Trinity Lutheran Church in Moorhead, Minnesota.

The Cooperative Baptist Fellowship (CBF) received grant funds to create residencies in ten churches. CBF and the church split the costs of the residency evenly over two years.

Be creative and take initiative, knowing that this is good and proven work that will benefit all parties. Judicatories tend to respond well to initiatives from their churches, while churches are slower to respond to judicatory initiatives.

Denominational bodies, no matter how creative and visionary, are often pressed for funds themselves. They may want to help but are limited financially. One possibility is to make an appeal for the assets of a church that is closing. When a church dwindles to the point that it cannot sustain continuing ministry as a viable congregation, it often has assets that result from the sale of property and possibly from unallocated endowment funds. When the church from which our church was birthed came to that point, the church treasurer came by my office to announce to me that he had just delivered a check to the Baptist Foundation that would be used for mission purposes. "With that check," he said, "our church did more today for the work of God than it has in many years." Similarly, another local Baptist church in Dallas has recently ceded its property to a newly created nonprofit organization for use by local benevolence ministries. The point is that churches are born and churches die. Everyone wants to be present at the birth, but those who are present at the death can help the church decide its legacy. Working with church and/or judicatory officials may produce fruit for pastoral residency.

SEMINARIES

Seeing their graduates succeed as well-trained pastors is the chief goal of seminaries. While they prepare students for work in chaplaincy, faith-based nonprofit work, and teaching in the academy, their founding purpose has always been and continues to be the preparation of the ministers. Some seminaries have forged partnerships with congregations to host their graduates in residencies that will continue the training of clergy and increase the likelihood of their success.

Virginia Theological Seminary (VTS) in Alexandria, Virginia, and McAfee School of Theology in Atlanta are two such examples. VTS is partnering with the Washington, D.C., cluster of Episcopal churches in a hybrid approach that bridges the last year of seminary and the first year of residency in a local parish. Churches seeking to begin residency programs of their own should explore relationships with the schools that educate their potential pastors. Trinity Lutheran has partnered with Concordia College and Luther Seminary to receive cash and in-kind gifts to strengthen their program. Pastor John Hulden says that a key to the partnership is mutual interest that leads to mutual benefit. Colleges and seminaries want relationships with young ministers. They need to understand the clergy they are training and the churches for which they are training clergy. Concordia and Luther have partnered with Trinity primarily by having professors go to the church periodically to work with residents. The church pays only their transportation costs. Concordia also hosts conferences for Trinity without charging them fees.

FOUNDATIONS

Foundations may be open to making grants to congregations that advance their goals of promoting religious work or improving clergy health. When researching foundations for the purpose of making proposals for grant funds, it is important to investigate the history of their grant making, the parameters they have established for funding, and the procedures they require for consideration.

Some denominations have foundations that support clergy well-being and leadership development. The Presbyterian Church (USA), the Christian Church (Disciples of Christ), and the Evangelical Lutheran Church of America are three examples. Framing a request for startup funds for a residency program that is in accordance with the aims of the foundation will help the request receive consideration. For example, we know that clergy burnout and the dropout rate of young clergy in the first five years are both chronic problems that concern denominations. A pastoral residency program addresses these challenges, but framing the request as a response to this concern might be a productive way of wording a grant request. Likewise, young pastors gain tremendous leadership skills during their residency time, and this might appeal to foundations interested in new models of leadership training. In the case of denominational foundations, grant requests that involve more than one congregation might increase their interest.

Some churches have foundations of their own that might be tapped for startup funds. One church that has begun a residency program received a grant for its program from its own foundation. The foundation makes grants for mission enterprises of and through their own church, and they deemed pastoral residency to be just that, a mission endeavor of the congregation. Few of these church foundations are set up to fund other churches, but they are perhaps the first place to look for possible startup and ongoing funding of a residency program in the church the foundation is attached to.

Some regional family foundations, such as the Cousins Foundation in Atlanta and the Duke Endowment in North Carolina have special interest in the work of Presbyterians and Methodists respectively in their areas. Family foundations are becoming more common as wealth is passed from one generation to another. People of means in local communities who have established these foundations are sometimes more flexible in their grant making than larger, more seasoned foundations. They might be interested in providing startup funds for something locally that they can see and experience up close.

Sustaining a Residency Program over Time

Once a residency program is up and running, plans must be set in motion to sustain the program for the long term. Several strategies can be employed simultaneously. Among those are the creation of a sinking fund in the budget, a restricted fund, an annual fund, and an endowment fund.

SINKING FUND

The concept of a sinking fund is most often used by governments and businesses to repay debt on bond issues or to buy back stock in the company. A sinking fund can also be employed by a local church. After the residency program is underway by means of startup funding, a church may begin to grow its budget gradually year by year to prepare itself to take over full responsibility for the program's cost.

In the case of a solo resident program, for instance, a church may estimate the total cost of the residency at $80,000 annually. If the church were to create a new line item in its budget for the program at $20,000 the first year, and then grow it over four years by adding $20,000 per year, the church would have the funds available to fully fund the residency program in two years' time. After two years, a total of $60,000 plus interest earned would be available out of savings from this sinking fund. That combined with another $20,000 from budget year three would fully fund the position that year. The remaining $40,000 in budget year three could be sent to savings, and then year four would be funded with 50 percent from savings and 50 percent from that year's budget. The calculus would change depending upon the rate of growth of the budget line item, the earnings on the sinking fund, and the time horizon determined. But the principle of growing the budget to reach full annual funding without having to do it all at once when startup funds are expended is nonetheless the same.

Trinity Lutheran Church in Moorhead has built its residency funding in this way. They have added $10,000 per year to a line item in their budget over eight years in order to insure that they will have the funds for an $80,000 per year resident at the end of that time. In the meantime, the annual sinking fund contribution of the budget has added up to a $360,000 commitment after four years that will support the program after foundation grants have expired.

RESTRICTED FUND

A fund could be established at the church separate from the operating budget that would allow people to contribute directly to the residency program. Donors would know that these monies are restricted to that end and would not be used for any other church purposes.

Wilshire has had good success in encouraging memorial gifts to our Pathways to Ministry Fund. When a loved one dies, the family may already know of the deceased's love for the residency work or might be encouraged to direct memorial gifts toward it rather than other programs of good will, such as cancer research or the heart association. Occasionally, someone might give a gift to this fund in honor of a staff anniversary or out of gratitude for a faithful Sunday school teacher. The important thing is to keep this fund before the people as an option for consideration by highlighting gifts made to it and how the funds are used. This fund may be the target of an operating budget sinking fund. The money in this fund may all be spent on the residency, unlike the way an endowment fund operates.

ANNUAL FUND

Another way to raise the capital for sustaining a residency is through an annual fund approach that asks people to subscribe year by year at various levels of giving. While this is more commonly used in educational and other nonprofit enterprises, something like a pastoral residency program might appeal to a congregation that can't raise the funds solely through the operating budget, from large gifts, or from outside sources. In this model, people would be asked at least once a year to contribute at suggested levels in order to keep the program going. While most church members will make the operating budget of the church their primary funding priority, many may also add to those gifts through the annual fund for pastoral residency. This may be seen as a competing interest with the budget, but it may also appeal to a generation that increasingly likes to give to direct causes more than to general funds. Like the sinking fund, these monies may be deposited in the restricted account and fully utilized to pay the expenses of the program.

ENDOWMENT FUND

The most effective long-term strategy for funding a pastoral residency program is the establishment of an endowment fund to pay for it in perpetuity. In this case, donors make gifts that will be invested for the purpose of growing the corpus of the fund over time. Since church endowment funds are not subject to mandatory annual distributions, the earnings can be added to the principal each year that the money is not needed. When the funds are needed, only the earnings on the fund would be used to pay for the program. A rule of thumb is that you should expect about 4 to 5 percent of the fund's value to be available annually, although fluctuations in markets may mean that more or less than that is available year to year. Because of that, a combination of funding strategies is encouraged that might include any or all of the above mentioned approaches.

Building a church endowment fund for pastoral residency can be achieved in two ways: (1) an endowment campaign and (2) a program of planned giving. Because of the popularity of Wilshire's residency, our church undertook an endowment campaign to fund the program for the future. A member who is passionate about the work hired a professional consultant to work with us in identifying potential donors and training a team of volunteers to present the case.[3] We actually delayed a building campaign for two years in order to make a priority of this stewardship effort. After talking with numerous members, we were able to raise $1.8 million over that two-year period. To fully fund our program from endowment will require more than six million dollars, but the campaign gave a good start to the endowment. The earnings on that money continue to grow the fund, and the success of that effort has given credibility and urgency to the funding plan. If no funds were available from other sources, the endowment would be able to pay for one resident, including program costs, from now on.

One of the best ways to appeal to people in this regard is by encouraging the gift of appreciated assets. If someone owns a stock or a piece of property that has appreciated in value, she may give that asset directly to the church and gain a double benefit in doing so. She will not pay tax on the amount the asset has appreciated, and she will get a tax deduction (subject to any IRS limitations) of the full amount of the gift. Many people buy and hold stock or real estate, and then they realize—generally later in life—that they will not need those assets to maintain their standard of living. Giving the assets charitably gives them a joy that holding onto them would not approach.

Another way to add to the endowment is through planned giving. If members designate the residency program—or the endowment fund—in their will, the bequests can add up quickly. Every church has members who have little or no family. When they die, there are often significant financial assets that must be disposed of in some manner. If members plan ahead as to how their estates will be divided at their death, the church's residency program can benefit. Members with large assets, who have already made plans for their family, may be looking for additional ways to bless the church beyond their lifetimes. Some have practiced faithful stewardship all their life, and the idea of being able to do so after their death is appealing.[4]

This is also true of closing churches, as described above. They will want to interpret their closing in language of living rather than dying. Appealing for long-term funding in addition to startup funds may be possible, depending upon the available resources. Significant giving to establish a residency program from residual funds after the closing of the church allows the church to speak of a kind of continuing life-after-death existence. One way to appeal for these funds is to name a resident position or the entire program (depending upon the size of the gift) for the defunct church. Churches that are closing want to believe that their mission will continue in some way. A naming opportunity will help to make that legacy more tangible.

Variations on endowment giving for individuals are gift annuities and charitable remainder trusts.[5] As an example of a gift annuity, a donor would enter into a contract with the church whereby he would give a certain amount to the church, and he would receive a charitable donation tax deduction for an amount in that year based upon an IRS calculation of the donor's life expectancy. The gift would become the church's property, in return for the church's promise to pay a defined benefit annually to the donor until the time of his death. This benefits both parties: the donor receives a tax donation, plus a guaranteed monthly income, which protects him from being subject to the vicissitudes of the market; the church will receive whatever is left of the value of the gift at the end of the donor's life. If the market performs better over the lifetime of the donor's annuity payments than the sum of those payments, then the value of the gift will be greater than when it was first given.[6] Charitable remainder trusts are similar, but the gift is transferred to a trust rather than the church. It is a more complex arrangement that requires legal assistance and usually involves contributions over $100,000.

⁓

Building the capital necessary to begin and sustain a residency program requires creativity and persistence. The best strategies are those that work best for each congregational culture. Consistent, ongoing attention to the work of securing adequate resources is critical to the long-term viability of the program.

Chapter 9

Binding Ties

Blest be the tie that binds
Our hearts in Christian love;
The fellowship of kindred minds
Is like to that above.

These felicitous lines from John Fawcett's hymn describe the
affection that churches and residents come to feel for one
another. When Wilshire residents conclude a vespers service,
they always do so by asking the church to join hands and sing
this stanza as a sending forth.

The conclusion of a resident's term brings the inevi-
table sending forth. The resident will go with the church's
blessing to serve in another place. But the hymn beauti-
fully depicts the bond of love that remains and the hope
of continued relationship across time. The residency church
and their resident alumni do well to commit themselves
to a continuation of mutual nurture. The church can still

share in the life of its former residents, and resident alumni can strengthen the residency church by continuing involvement with the program they left behind. This mutuality of blessing may take various forms. On the church's side, it may involve creating communication channels for residents past and present to stay in touch, providing coaching help, supporting peer groups and ongoing networks of young ministers, and hosting reunions and other events that bring residents back to the host church. On the resident alumni side, it may mean honoring the relationship with the residency church by staying in contact, helping in the recruitment and placement of residents that come behind them, and returning for church-sponsored events. The relationship created by the time of residency bears long-term covenantal possibility. Nurturing that ongoing relationship begins the moment residents leave for their first call.

Transition Help

When the resident leaves for her first call, she is leaving behind some relationships that have become important to her and to those she is leaving. Residency creates opportunities for closeness with staff, resident peers, and lay leadership that abruptly change when the resident leaves. Just as the whole residency has been an effort to aid the transition into ministry, so this move from the residency church to the first call congregation is a crucial transition. The calling church will be welcoming the new minister with joy and hospitality, but the sending church can play a part too—not by holding on in a codependent way, but by letting go with continuing grace.

For instance, the sending church might write a letter of commendation to the calling church, wishing a blessing on this new ministry and pledging its prayers. Wilshire always contacts the calling church and provides altar flowers in honor of the first Sunday of the new ministry. The Village Church in Wellesley sends their Oversight Committee to visit former residents at their new church, worship with them, and share a meal. In family systems terms, this "binds anxiety" that might build up due to the physical distance between the two churches and the shifting of relationship priorities. It helps to prevent "emotional cutoff" that might sabotage the transition.

Another gift that the sending church might consider is to share with the calling church the cost of a coach for the new minister over the first two years. This can be done either by the sending church paying the first year and asking the calling church to pick up the second year, or by sharing the cost from the beginning. Wilshire has made this arrangement both ways: one church took up the entire cost of the coaching for their new pastor as a result of our suggestion, while two other churches agreed to share the cost. Either way, coaching aids the new pastor after the mentoring tether is cut.

As discussed earlier, the movement from mentoring to coaching is appropriate at this transition. A coach is an experienced leadership counselor who will give feedback to the new minister and help him find solutions to ministry challenges that draw upon his own wisdom and resources. A coach doesn't say what she would do if she were he in that circumstance; she helps the new minister to discover the path that fits him best based on who he is.

Fostering Networks of Support

Residents have learned to live and work in community. They value collegiality. One area of concern for departing residents is whether they will be able to sustain the collegial culture they are leaving behind in the residency. Generally, the answer is "no." Residents should steel themselves for that new reality, so that it doesn't surprise them when they go to a congregation or staff that doesn't understand this approach to ministry. This is especially true for residents who go to associate pastor positions and find that they are working for a senior pastor who does not foster a supportive culture for the staff.

There are ways to address this ahead of time and mitigate its sting. First, residents should be honest in the interviewing process about their desire to serve in a church with a collaborative staff culture. They may need to outline what that would mean to the search committee, and they may need to probe other staff members at the church to get a good read on the culture. Knowing what they are going to will allow them to enter with their eyes open. Second, residents can contribute to changing the culture in their first call church. Some churches don't know what they are missing because they haven't experienced it. Residents will bring with them to their new church a vision of how a church can function collaboratively and supportively. Finally, residents can look beyond the staff of their new church for peer groups of support. Dallas has an ecumenical peer group for women ministers—Christian ministers and Jewish rabbis—that meets regularly with a professional counselor who has created a safe space for them. Peer groups are flourishing in many denominations, and they are usually created by motivated young

ministers. Residency churches can raise these possibilities for
the departing residents and sometimes advocate with the new
church or the denomination on their behalf.

Peer Groups

Resident alumni can continue to develop collegial relationships through peer groups. Some denominations and
judicatories facilitate peer groups for clergy that provide an
antidote to isolation and encouragement in the work. The
Episcopal Diocese of Chicago links new solo pastors in a
colleague group for the first three years, and the mentor/
rector from their two-year curate (intern/resident) program
continues with them during this time. The new ministers
meet every six weeks in the smaller colleague groups and
then gather once a year with the larger Making Excellent
Disciples participants. The Cooperative Baptist Fellowship
has made a priority of connecting ministers through its
peer network. Clergy peer groups are initiated by ministers
and facilitated by Fellowship staff. Groups are self-directed,
with one minister coordinating the group. The Fund for
Theological Education makes vocational friendship grants
of $1,000 for up to two years for former residents who want
to create peer groups.[1] Although these grants are only open
to former residents from the Transition into Ministry (TiM)
community, former residents from non-TiM programs may
join a group formed by one of these grants.

The Massachusetts Conference of the United Church
of Christ (UCC) has exported its learnings in new clergy
development from the pastoral residency program of
the Wellesley church not only to all of Massachusetts but
also to UCC conferences in Vermont, Rhode Island, and

Connecticut. They all now require that new clergy be part of a New Clergy Group. The testimony of those involved in such groups bears witness to the effect. One participant says, "My group has been a great resource for defining and answering practical questions—both those I might think of ahead of time, and also questions that arise in the course of our conversations." These include things such as: How often should a pastor meet with the church moderator? If you're officiating Ash Wednesday by yourself, do you put ashes on your own forehead, or have a layperson do it? What should one do about a particularly frustrating situation? Should a pastor be called by first name, by title (Reverend or Doctor), or a combination, such as Pastor Jane or Pastor Smith? How does a pastor address a suicide in conversation with the surviving family and in the funeral homily?

Questions like these move back and forth from things more or less spiritually consequential, but they are all concerns that come up in the pastoral life and a clergy peer group is a good place to address them. "There is always at least one person who seems to be in a similar situation, and the others are quick to empathize. Sometimes they have already dealt with my situation and have come through the other side, so their wisdom and counsel is particularly helpful." Experienced pastors facilitate each group, and this strengthens their ministries and churches also, while giving them renewed hope for the future of the church. "What a delight," reports one such pastor, "to be able to encourage excellence in the practice of ministry and be of assistance in discerning the movement of the Spirit in their lives and ministries!"[2]

Social Media

In addition to the residency pastor and other key persons from the sending church remaining in contact with the resident in the months and years that follow the departure from the program, the use of social media to create virtual community can help to maintain the connection. A "closed" Facebook group will allow current and former residents, along with the senior pastor and program administrator, to remain in touch.[3] Younger people are adept at using social media to share comforts and cares, hopes and fears. Or as Fawcett puts it in stanza three of his hymn:

> We share each other's woes,
> our mutual burdens bear;
> and often for each other flows
> the sympathizing tear.

Residents can ask each other questions about how to handle things they encounter for the first time, announce engagements, marriages, births, and ask for prayer. They can share books and articles, pictures and videos, job opportunities and future resident recommendations. It can become an ongoing community of support that is anchored in the hospitality and generosity of the residency church.

The Fund for Theological Education, which oversees the residency programs funded by the Lilly Endowment, has created a closed Facebook group for those who have participated in residency programs across the country. While it is an "invitation only" group, resident alumni from non-Lilly funded programs are welcome to join. This site keeps new ministers aware of resources available to them through FTE and elsewhere. Articles are posted that aid in ongoing learning. Discussions about theological subjects and ministry practices keep young ministers informed and engaged with peers that have gone through similar ministry formation.

Reunions and Retreats

So far we have looked at how the residency church might continue to encourage the success of their former residents. We have also talked about how residents might continue to grow through peer learning. Periodic residency reunions can serve the dual purposes of peer learning and strengthening the residency program of the home church.

Some churches host annual reunions, while others do so every two years or only occasionally. By returning to their residency churches, young ministers get to tell stories to church members about how the residency has helped them in their first call. This reinforces to the church the value of the program. It also helps to make the case to those who might be financial supporters of the program. Returning residents may meet with their former lay support team, preach on a Sunday, teach a Sunday school class or Wednesday Bible study, meet with program leaders and staff, and enjoy social time with current residents.

The reunion solidifies the peer community among those who have gone through the program and with those currently doing so. Current residents often report on how encouraging this time is for them, since their forebears in the program have taken the steps they will soon take into first call churches.

In some years Wilshire has brought in seminary professors, experienced pastors, or writers to lead sessions that make the time a continuing education experience. This ingredient makes it possible for some of them to expense a portion of the trip to their budgets for church conferences. Increasingly, however, resident alumni consider the time spent learning from one another to be the greatest value of the reunion. One outgrowth of these reunions among our residents is that they begin to invite each other to their churches, and they partner with one another's churches for joint mission projects.

Another way to strengthen the bonds between the church and its former residents is by inviting them to lead retreats for the home church. Churches typically plan women's retreats, spiritual formation weekends, senior adult events, and youth camps. All these are possible leadership opportunities for former residents to contribute to their former church and demonstrate their growth in ministry.

⁓

The fourth stanza of "Blest Be the Tie That Binds" summarizes the spirit and desire of nurturing the ongoing relationship between residency church and resident alumni across time:

When we asunder part,
It gives us inward pain;
But we shall still be joined in heart,
And hope to meet again.

Conclusion

"Can I Get a Witness?"

This book began by urging you to consider whether starting a pastoral residency program was the right choice for your church. Since you've read this far, you're still considering the value of the undertaking. The good news is that you would not be the first if you choose to move forward. Others have piloted this work and learned—by trial and error, by practice and success—that the benefits are immense to all involved.

As a preacher might say to the congregation when trying to emphasize his point, "Can I get a witness?" Yes, we have witnesses. Residents who have gone through the program and are now serving as pastors have a word. So do those serving in the host churches as clergy and lay mentors. Even those who haven't had a direct connection to a pastoral residency program but have longed for the renewal of the church in our time bear witness to the hope of this work for the future.

A New Generation of Competent and Confident Pastors

Ministry is a lifelong practice. A pastoral residency program accelerates the learning by providing an incubation period for fledgling ministers. They develop a full repertoire of skills and bank experiences from which they will draw in the years to come. The testimonies of those who have gone through these programs bear witness to the value of this work in their future ministry.

Andrew Daugherty, serving the Myers Park Baptist Church in Charlotte, North Carolina, says of his residency: "This experience of being trusted with liturgical leadership, pastoral care, staff collaboration, and teaching inspired a fuller trust in my own pastoral competencies. The residency did not create these competencies as much as it supplied a practicing and reflective context in which to discover them and deepen them." God gives the gifts, but the church helps a minister discover and develop those gifts for ministry.

Jana Reister is serving the Knox Presbyterian Church in Cincinnati, Ohio, now, something she could not have imagined doing without the residency: "As my two years came to a close, the fear about church/pulpit ministry remained, but I claimed my gifts for church ministry, including preaching—gifts I became aware of through the residency. So, fear and all, I followed God's lead and pursued an associate pastor position (again, I knew I wanted/needed colleagues). I am flourishing and learning to stop digging in my heels to living into the leader God created me to be. The less I resist, the more I flourish and the better God can use me as an instrument of God's grace, peace, love and healing."

Anne Jernberg, pastor of Calvary Baptist Church in Denver, Colorado, agrees: "The weight of its worth is in the affirmation of call that the congregation instills in your voice from the pulpit, your posture at the bedside, your mind during tedious meetings and crucial conversations (both), your hands through the breaking of bread and baptism, and your heart in those moments when you wonder if you're even called in the first place." That last part goes to one reason the whole Transition into Ministry came into being. Too many young ministers leave church work in the first five years of service.[1] Although the data isn't complete yet, residency seems to instill resilience in young pastors that allows them to push through difficult times in ministry.

Another young minister, Ryan Heritage of the First Baptist Church in Clinton, Tennessee, points to the stretching of pastoral imagination: "By being in the residency, we were able to know full details of common and uncommon situations, how they happened, and what path was taken to resolve them. A majority of the time, the correct path was taken by our mentors because of who they are; and they are good at it. However, when the wrong path was taken, they would share with us what they did wrong and share another solution that would have probably worked better." This likewise had a dual effect: first, seeing the successes allowed residents to develop what Ryan calls "muscle memory," that is, a kind of instinct for ministry; and second, witnessing the failures reflectively taught them that they may learn from mistakes and not become defensive about them. Even experienced ministers err, but giving and receiving grace within the community has a long-term positive impact on the minister and the church.

"The crucial work in the early years of ministry," says Clarence Langdon, Director of the Making Excellent Disciples program of the Episcopal Diocese of Chicago, "is learning how to read a congregation, understand its DNA, and cast a vision for mission that engages that congregation for effective and faithful ministry." Residency allows young pastors to work alongside experienced pastors in developing their capacity to "read and lead" congregations. This helps young pastors develop "practical intelligence," as Malcolm Gladwell puts it in his provocative book *Outliers*. It includes things like "knowing what to say to whom, knowing when to say it, and knowing how to say it for maximum effect."[2]

An alumnus of the program at St. James' Church in New York expressed his gratitude with incarnational imagery: "God made the Word flesh, and St. James' made instruction experiential." Residency ties together theory and practice with a bond that would be missing without both seminary and residency.

Another lingering experience of residencies that somehow surprises young pastors is having a community that cheers for them and follows them in the years ahead. It's like having a fan club that follows them on the road, not just at home. Matthew Marston, pastor of Trinity Baptist Church in Moultrie, Georgia, explains: "The residency gives us a *ministerial* home church in a way that is especially helpful. It is difficult for childhood churches to bless young ministers in a robust way. The residency congregation gives us a place of support and care that is behind us wherever we are. We get the blessing of not just being called, but sent."

Finally, Anne Jernberg again: The creation of a "network of collegiality and ongoing mentoring multiplies exponentially year by year as the congregation continues to call, nurture, and equip more and more residents." Pastors need friends for the journey. Residency goes beyond seminary by narrowing the peer learning to a more focused group of lifelong colleagues who share language and experience that larger groups lack. Having companions to check with and to encourage in good times and bad promotes clergy well being for years to come.

Congregations that Become
Vibrant Learning Communities

The seven last words of the church—not to be confused with the seven last words of Jesus from the cross—are, "We've never done it that way before." Right, but why? Churches often stagnate by failing to distinguish between tradition and traditionalism. As the late Yale historian Jaroslav Pelikan put it: "Tradition is the living faith of the dead; traditionalism is the dead faith of the living. Tradition lives in conversation with the past, while remembering where we are and when we are and that it is we who have to decide. Traditionalism supposes that nothing should ever be done for the first time, so all that is needed to solve any problem is to arrive at the supposedly unanimous testimony of this homogenized tradition."[3]

The principle *ecclesia reformata, semper reformata* means that the Reformation Church is always reforming itself. It's not enough for Protestant churches to be faithful to the roots of their traditions by only doing what their founders did.[4] They must continue to learn and work out the meaning of the gospel for their time. Thus innovation and tradition are not set against one another; they are actually partners in one great enterprise of a living faith.[5]

A church-based pastoral residency program helps the church sharpen its ministry. Residents ask the church why it does things the way it does. They learn to appreciate the tradition and to become part of it. In seminary they learn about the theological river of orthodoxy and their own denominational tributary of it. But in residency training they wade into the waters by learning the practices that flow from those sources. At the same time, they help the church to become self-conscious about its practices. Pastors and lay leaders have to explain why they do what they do, and sometimes this nudges the church to cut a fresh path.

For example, the Wellesley church reports that "from the beginning of our program, we had imagined that it might serve as yeast in the dough of the whole congregation, encouraging us to explore ways to be more intentional not only about pastoral formation, but also about Christian formation." They have revised their confirmation program for young people in light of the learning from residency work, and they have seen the need to help all Christians affirm their vocation as the people of God—"identifying gifts, discerning God's call, and claiming a ministry." At Wilshire we have learned that lay support teams help all new staff as they make their way into the congregation over the first two years. Moreover, Sunday school teachers and other lay leaders are learning to mentor younger members to share in their work more effectively as they step into leadership roles.

Because a residency program demands the attention of the entire staff and the time and energy of the congregation, Chris Braudaway-Bauman of the Wellesley church echoes the testimony of other residency churches: "We have been delighted to discover that as we help them grow in ministry, we grow in new ways ourselves."

Lewis Galloway is the Senior Minister of the Second Presbyterian Church in Indianapolis, the church that pioneered pastoral residency work. Although he inherited the program, he has witnessed firsthand its impact on the church. "The residency program has transformed the life of our congregation. The residents have helped us be more intentional about growing into our identity as a community of teaching and learning. The residents bring passion, fresh ideas, and a willingness to take risks. The congregation is eager to encourage the residents, support their ideas and programs, listen to their teaching, and, when necessary, even challenge their assumptions. It is a joy to watch the residents and congregation flourish in ministry together. The residency program, more than any other ministry of the church, has led our congregation see itself as a community of faith that mentors spiritual leadership for the church, family, community, and world."

The Renewal of the Church in America

The ultimate goal of a congregational pastoral residency is greater than the training of any individual minister or the vitalizing of any single church. It is nothing less than the renewal of every church that will be touched by this work for generations to come. Imagine your church being part of a movement of God's Spirit that will renew hundreds of churches in America.

Every year Wilshire publishes a map of the United States with dots all over the map that have lines connecting back to Dallas. After a decade of residency work, there are nineteen dots on that map. The congregation knows that in the years to come there will be many places they travel to that will have a former Wilshire resident preaching that next Sunday. What's more, when members move or young people go off to college, we will have greater confidence in the churches we recommend to them if one of our alumni is serving there.

Now multiply that phenomenon by the number of churches that have already engaged this work, and then add your own. Within a generation of churches like yours taking up the task of training young ministers, the church in America may find itself healthier and happier in its service of the world for Christ, being led by pastors who have added wisdom to knowledge.

An elderly member of Church of the Servant in Grand Rapids, Michigan, retired from his own lifelong work as a missionary, commented about the special work of the church's residents with immigrants and refugees: "What a joy to me to have watched them blossom, as it were, into a mature woman and man of God, and become skilled in the ministries of outreach and assimilation. The Lord has a bright future for them—and for his church!" While that might have been true anyway, whether they had served as pastoral residents or not, the evidence of their growth through the residency program gives greater weight to their promise as ministers. Church of the Servant residency program administrator, Dale Cooper, believes that "life is lived forward, but learned backward." When older and more experienced ministers transmit their learning successfully to those who will lead the church into the future, the future church will be stronger for it.

David Wood, Senior Minister of the Glencoe Union Church on the North Shore of Lake Michigan in the Chicago area, was the national coordinator for pastoral residency work among the churches and institutions during the first decade of the movement. He summarizes the impact well: "The ministry is essentially a practice. If we lose our capacity to teach ministry in and through practice, we will lose an essential dimension of how the practice of ministry endures and thrives over time—how it gets passed from one generation to the next. It is this process of transmission through practice that also keeps practitioners alive to their craft and novices alert to how their expertise depends in no small measure upon the wisdom of those who have gone before. If this process of transmission breaks down, the practice of leadership becomes overly responsive to the currents of the day and unhinged from the tradition that funds its integrity. By keeping this transmission process hinged to the tradition through models of mentoring like congregation-based residency, hope for the renewal of the larger church becomes all the more buoyant."

To think on such a large scale, however, requires that church leaders be mature enough to act strategically, even if the impact of their actions is truly known after they themselves are gone. The late pastor of the Riverside Church in New York, Ernest Campbell, famously said, "To be young is to study in schools we did not build. To be mature is to build schools in which we will not study. To be young is to swim in pools we did not dig. To be mature is to dig pools in which we will not swim. To be young is to sit under trees we did not plant. To be mature is to plant trees under which we will not sit. To be young is to dance to music we did not write. To be mature is to write music to which we will not dance."[6] Adding to this, church historian Walter B. Shurden says, "To be young is to benefit from a church you did not begin; to be mature is to build a church from which you will not benefit."[7]

Notes

Introduction—The Role of the Congregation in Training Clergy

1. This will be described more fully in the first chapter, but the concept of churches as communities of shared practices is well chronicled by James P. Wind and David J. Wood in their important introductory work *Becoming a Pastor: Reflections on the Transition into Ministry* (An Alban Institute Special Report, 2008).
2. "Thoughts on the *Transition into Ministry* Program," an unpublished address to the program leaders of the churches and denominations engaged in this work (February 2005).
3. Holly G. Miller, "Easing the Transition: From Seminary to Parish Ministry," in *Congregations* (Alban: Jan./Feb. 2002): 11.
4. Christina Starace, former resident of Second Presbyterian Church, Indianapolis, in Miller, "Easing the Transition": 11.
5. Competence and confidence are two important goals of pastoral resident training. "Easing the Transition from Seminary to Congregation," Lilly Endowment Annual Report, Religion Division (2001), 51.
6. The Fund for Theological Education web site, http://www.fteleaders. org/pages/callingcongregations, is a rich resource for churches that want to do the work of identifying and encouraging the call to ministry in young people.
7. A comprehensive account of how field education is approached by three seminaries is found in *Educating Clergy: Teaching Practices and Pastoral Imagination* by Charles R. Foster, Lisa E. Dahill, Lawrence A. Golemon, and Brabara Wang Tolentino (Jossey-Bass, 2006), especially chapter 10: "Cultivating Professional Practices: Field Education."

Chapter 1—*Assessing Readiness*

1. Bruce C. McIver, *Riding the Wind of God: A Personal History of the Youth Revival Movement* (Smyth and Helwys, 2002).
2. Neena Stija, *The Dallas Morning News* (August 3, 2010): 1A, 12A.

Chapter 2—*Customizing a Model*

1. Although the intention of this resource is to make it less necessary for a church to do all its own legwork in researching models for a potential program, contacting churches and key leaders personally is still advised. One of the joys of those who do this work is helping others undertake it too.
2. Many pastoral residents graduate from their programs to accept callings to associate roles in churches initially, but they are at least prepared for the possibility that they will become senior pastors at some future time.
3. Most churches will likely find it to be good policy not to hire residents as full-time staff after their residency is completed. To do so might undermine the concept of training them for the wider Church and sending them out to serve. It might also create false expectations in future residents who might see the resident role as a trial period rather than a transition period.
4. Providence Baptist Church in Charlotte, North Carolina, has used the young adult example, while First Baptist Church in Madison, Alabama, has employed a variant of the children's ministry model.
5. One additional example of this correlation might be with a church that calls its second or third permanent staff member. Expectations are often high from the congregation, but the person called may be young and have little experience in ministry. If the church were to surround the new staff member with a residency-like team of laypersons and accept the challenge of being a teaching congregation with this new minister, the church and the young minister may have a more successful transition. Our own church has followed this

pattern with a young minister who asked for this kind of support in her role as adult minister. She is the same age as our residents and saw the kind of formation they were receiving. This experience has helped us to reevaluate how we receive new staff generally and help them assimilate into the culture of the church.

6. Mentoring and coaching are two different things: a mentor tends to teach the resident what he would do in a given situation; a coach would try to draw out the best wisdom of the young minister himself. The Center for Congregational Health in Winston-Salem, North Carolina, is an excellent resource for ministerial coaching. Peer learning groups are a growing phenomenon within denominations, as ministers find they are learning from one another in small, covenant groups that meet periodically and often read and discuss books and articles.

7. Cohorts of four residents at a time in classes of two residents per year seems to be the largest effective number. Churches that have tried to do five have cut back to four, and churches that have gone to three residents have changed their pattern to classes of three or fewer that come in together and stay for two years, thus eliminating the staggered class approach.

8. Some churches that employ this pattern include Wellesley Congregational Church in Wellesley, Massachusetts, Central Christian Church in Lexington, KY, and St. Paul's Lutheran Church in Davenport, Iowa. Central Presbyterian Church in Atlanta, GA, has reshaped its residency into overlapping three-year terms. One resident enters each year for three years. By staggering three classes of one resident each over a longer period, they believe residents will be better prepared when they leave and will have left a stronger legacy by their ministry at the residency church.

9. Chapter 8 on Building Capital will address in more detail that development of a budget and business plan that will aid in projecting costs.

10. A common English paraphrase of the original Scottish dialect in "To a Mouse."

Chapter 3—Forming the Team

1. "Pastoral and Ecclesial Imagination," in Dorothy C. Bass and Craig Dykstra, eds., *For Abundant Life: Practical Theology, Education, and Christian Ministry* (Eerdmans, 2008), 54–55.
2. The expansion of the mentoring component to newly ordained clergy in the Massachusetts Conference has now spread to Vermont, Connecticut, and Rhode Island. This is just one example of how what is learned in resident mentoring continues to find new applications in other venues.
3. Albert L. Winseman, *Living Your Strengths: Discover Your Gof-Given Talents, and Inspire Your Congregation and Community* (Gallup Organization, 2003).

Chapter 4— Recruiting Residents

1. Howard Gardner, *Multiple Intelligences: New Horizons in Theory and Practice* (Basic Books, 1993, 2006), and Daniel Goleman, *Emotional Intelligence: Why It Matters More Than IQ* (Bantam, 1996, 2006).
2. *The Best and the Brightest* (Random House, 1969).
3. Most churches see the wisdom in choosing residents in their mid-twenties to mid-thirties, which gives them a time horizon for ministry that will have long-lasting effect for the Church. Second-career ministers bless many churches, but their late start means they have fewer years to offer for the investment made by residency churches.
4. Two exceptions might be noted to this idea of desiring clarity of call in resident candidates. Sometimes women might be slower to own a pastoral call, because they have not seen female role models in the pulpit in their tradition or been encouraged to consider God's call to be a pastor. The residency might be just the thing a woman minister needs to own her call, as the church will affirm, perhaps for the first time, that she has the gifts and graces for this work. If a church considers part of its charge to strengthen the diversity of the pastors it sends out, it will call women to be residents and accept

the fact that they may need more work in adopting pastoral identity than their male counterparts. Another possible exception might be gay and lesbian candidates. While some Protestant churches have been advocates for the full inclusion of gay and lesbian persons in church membership, fewer have been advocates for their inclusion in ordained pastoral roles.

5. "Cultivating a Pastoral Imagination," unpublished address to fellows of the Fund for Theological Education (June 22, 2002). Used with permission. What I am calling "markers" are in Wiginton's nomenclature "markers of resistance." Her point is to juxtapose the qualities of those who may be good candidates for ministry over against those who seem to adopt the values of the dominant culture. For our purposes these can be positively stated simply to convey the prompts to look for in potential residents. With gratitude for her insights, I have restated them and described them in my own words.

6. *A Slender Grace: Poems* (Eerdmans, 2004). The preface makes good reading for any preacher. He coins the term "incarnality" to describe the particularity with which poets (and preachers) should attend to things and to speak of things.

7. "Guide Me, O Thou Great Jehovah," words by William Williams.

8. Back Bay Books, 2007.

Chapter 5—Simulating Ministry

1. Pastors in the Methodist itinerate system are deliberately moved from parish to parish more often than in other polities, and pastors who know they will be leaving a church—whether for another ministry or for retirement—may all profit by the end of residency experience that is otherwise unusual.

2. Because of the difficulty in timing a resident's exit with a matching call, most programs try to set minimum expectations of about 21 months' service in order to assure adequate time for pastoral formation. While some residents may leave the program early, others may come to the end of their residency without securing a pastoral call.

It is unadvisable to extend the residency time by continuing the program, because it will interfere with the pattern of welcome and integration of new residents. But there may be ways to create special assignments for the resident on a month-by-month basis that will allow him or her to make contributions to the church or the residency while still searching for a pastoral position.

Chapter 6—Designing the Program

1. Malcolm Gladwell, *Outliers: The Story of Success* (Little, Brown and Company, 2008).
2. Based on a rough estimate of ten hours of sermon preparation times fifty sermons per year, which yields twenty years of preaching to optimize the craft.
3. "Unplanned Ministry: Being Jackson's Pastor," *Christian Century* (February 8, 2011): 32-34.
4. Louis Weeks, *All for God's Glory: Redeeming Church Scutwork* (Alban Institute, 2008), 6.
5. Weeks, 14.
6. Annual report to the Lilly Endowment, January 29, 2010.

Chapter 7—Prodding Progress

1. www.faithandleadership.com/blog/08-03-2011/james-howell-evaluation-anxiety.
2. *Twelve Keys to an Effective Church* (Jossey-Bass, 1997).
3. Author unknown. http://www.jazzshelf.org/blakey.html.
4. Alban Institute, 2004.
5. A copy of this can be found and adapted from the Wilshire website (www.wilshirebc.org/pathwaysdallas) or at the TiM website (www.fteleaders.org).
6. Several residency churches have built into their program a 6-month trial period, at which time the resident and the church have the option to discontinue the relationship without recrimination. In this case, it helps to schedule a 3-month check-up conversation with

every resident so that there are no surprises when the six-month review takes place.

7. A comprehensive website that includes introduction to appreciative inquiry and many applications of it is through Case Western University's Weatherhead School of Management, http://appreciativeinquiry.case.edu/. A short book that might be helpful is David L. Cooperrider and Diana Whitney, *Appreciative Inquiry: A Positive Revolution in Change* (Berrett-Koehler, 2005).

8. These may be found in the same places as the 360-degree instrument discussed above.

Chapter 8—Building Capital

1. Costs in the first year will be greater than the following year or years, due to recruitment and moving expenses, as well as initial office setup costs.

2. Even so-called permanent staff move on and must be replaced from time to time, but the average tenure of permanent staff will likely be much longer than the two- or three-year service of a resident.

3. In my experience the senior pastor is the best person to present the case to and ask for contributions from potential givers. If the pastor has experience in previous campaigns, he or she can organize a team to carry out this work without the aid of a consultant.

4. One question many donors to endowment funds ask (or don't ask, but should have answered anyway) is what happens to their gift if things change. What if the church decides no longer to operate a residency program? What happens if the church changes so much in character over time that the donor's confidence is lost? Provisions can be made in the endowment agreement as to what would happen to the funds in the event the church discontinued the program. Most often donors are satisfied to know that some church-elected committee will be able to reallocate those funds to purposes akin to the spirit of the gift. In the latter case of the church changing theologically or philosophically, little assurances can be made to donors. There is always a

measure of faith in any gift. Donors lose control of their gift once it is given. They should understand at the time of their decision that the gift is given "as unto the Lord" more than to the church.

5. The church should enlist the help of a financial professional to explain fully these somewhat complicated legal instruments for planned giving. The primary difference between a gift annuity and a charitable remainder trust is that the former is contractual and the latter fiduciary. A church is required to make the payments to the annuitant, even if the value of the fund from the original gift is depleted. Under the general rubric of a charitable remainder trust, the payments are made to the annuitant in ways that are calculated either on the value of the fund at the first of each year (unitrust), or until the funds in the trust are completely expended and not beyond (remainder trust).

6. The only caution with a gift annuity is that the church's obligation to pay the annuitant could outrun the gift if the annuitant were to live longer than the actuaries estimate. For this reason, the church should have assets in reserve to cover such a situation.

Chapter 9—Binding Ties

1. Information and application form are available at the FTE site for Transition into Ministry. www.fteleaders.org/pages/TiM-05.

2. From the 2010 Program Report to the Lilly Endowment from the Massachusetts Conference of the United Church of Christ.

3. A "closed" group means that only those who are invited to join may see and make posts to the group. Privacy matters. Residents will share more freely if the space created is safe for their honest communications.

Conclusion—"Can I Get a Witness?"

1. Church consultant Kennon Callahan claims that one in five clergy in new positions are effective almost immediately, another one in five fail in the first six months, and three out of five are potentially effective pastors that require, along with their congregations, a lot of work.

Pastoral residency aims to strengthen the "naturals," and develop the capacities of those among the 60 percent who with coaching and mentoring have the capacity for excellence. See *Twelve Keys to an Effective Church* (Jossey-Bass, 1983).

2. *Outliers: The Story of Success* (Little, Brown and Company, 2008).
3. Valerie R. Hotchkiss, Patrick Henry, and Jarolav Jan Pelikan, eds., *Orthodoxy and Western Culture: A Collection of Essays Honoring Jaroslav Pelikan on His Eightieth Birthday* (St. Vladamir's Seminary, 2006).
4. By Protestant Church I mean to include also those churches that grew out of the Anabaptist and Separatist traditions too, although strictly speaking they were historically different movements. Thus Baptist and Mennonite churches, along with Christian churches—Disciples, Church of Christ, and Independent Christian churches—all share this principle of being ever-reforming communities of faith.
5. C. Kavin Rowe has coined the felicitous phrase "traditioned innovation" to describe the church's pattern of following the work of the creative and redeeming God of scripture. www.faithandleadership. duke.edu/content/traditioned-innovation-biblical-way-thinking.
6. "Hanging Back," a sermon preached at Riverside, July 8, 1973.
7. "Judson and Rice Talk to Moderate Baptists," April 22, 2005. www. centerforbaptiststudies.org/shurden/under.htm.